THE ULTIMATE SCI-FI MOVIE QUIZ BOOK

First published in the UK in 2024 by Studio Press,
an imprint of Bonnier Books UK,
4th Floor, Victoria House, Bloomsbury Square,
London WC1B 4DA
Owned by Bonnier Books, Sveavägen 56, Stockholm,
Sweden

www.bonnierbooks.co.uk

1 3 5 7 9 10 8 6 4 2

ISBN 978-1-80078-939-5

MIX
Paper | Supporting responsible forestry
FSC® C018072

Written by Chris Farnell
Edited by Frankie Jones
Cover designed by Maddox Philpot
Designed by Nathan Balsom and Alessandro Susin
Production by Giulia Caparrelli

A CIP catalogue record for this book is available
from the British Library

Printed and bound in Great Britain by Clays Ltd,
Elcograf S.p.A

THE ULTIMATE SCI-FI MOVIE QUIZ BOOK

STUDIO PRESS

CONTENTS

INTRODUCTION

We love science fiction because it opens up a universe of possibilities – alien planets, other dimensions, vistas of time and space. It is a place where we can meet strange alien life forms, hyperintelligent machines, infernal mad scientists, and perhaps most importantly, ourselves (but evil, and with a goatee).

From the depths of Frankenstein's laboratory to the distant sands of Arrakis, science fiction films have shown us countless wonders.

But more than that, science fiction has always been a genre about asking questions – the big questions that have baffled philosophers, scientists and thinkers since the dawn of humanity.

Are we alone in the universe?

Where might we end up if society continues along its current path?

How might history have turned out differently?

What, ultimately, is it that makes us truly human?

And which comedic detective was played by the same actor as the flying saucer captain in Forbidden Planet?

Within the pages of this book, you will find the answer to precisely one of these questions.

But some questions are harder than others. If you're a science fiction movie novice, you'll want to start with our Caveman-level questions for each quiz. If you consider your science fiction movie knowledge to be a bit more evolved, the Astronaut-level questions are for you. Then again, if your science fiction movie knowledge has transcended its material form to become a being of pure energy, the Pan-Dimensional Star Baby-level questions will really test you.

ROBOTS AND AI

The word 'robot' is barely more than a hundred years old, but the concept predates modern science fiction as we know it. Its roots go back beyond *Frankenstein* and the chess-playing 'Mechanical Turk' hoax, to the myth of the Golem, or Homer's Iliad where we find "handmaidens wrought of gold in the semblance of living maids".

For as long as we have built machines, we have noticed that, actually, humans look a bit like machines, and from there, it's a short leap to realising we can make machines like humans. Machines that will do everything we say and, most importantly, never rise up and kill us all.

HUMANOID ROBOTS

If you're building a robot, why mess with a classic design? Two arms, two legs, one head, free will, it's a classic combination. The problems start when robots are a bit too good at looking like humans, and you don't know whether your best friend is a robot. Then the real problems start when you don't know if you are a robot...

1. *Westworld (1973)* shows us a Wild West theme park overrun by killer robot cowboys. But what was the other deadly theme park its writer is known for?

2. In *The Stepford Wives (1975)*, Katharine Ross discovers a plan to replace her with a robot housewife - but who replaces her as the star of the film's 2004 remake?

   A: Scarlett Johansson
   B: Angelina Jolie
   C: Nicole Kidman
   D: Halle Berry

3. Roy Batty, the rogue replicant from *Blade Runner (1982)*, has seen things you wouldn't believe. Name one of the things he has seen that you would not believe.

4. In *The Terminator (1984)*, only John Connor can destroy Skynet, but who is John Connor's dad?

   A: Kyle Reese
   B: Todd Voight
   C: Benjamin Schantz
   D: Matt Buchanan

5. In *Terminator 2: Judgment Day (1991)*, Sarah and John Connor, with some help from a friendly Terminator, prevent Skynet's war on humanity. But on what date was Judgement Day supposed to happen?

   A: 29 August 1997
   B: 31 December 1999
   C: 21 December 2012
   D: 15 January 2021

6. In *Bill & Ted's Bogus Journey (1991)*, the only thing that can defeat two evil robot duplicates are two good robot duplicates. But who built the good robot duplicates?
   A: Albert Einstein
   B: Station
   C: The Grim Reaper
   D: Marilyn Monroe

7. In *Bicentennial Man (1999)*, what name does the robot NDR, played by Robin Williams, choose for himself?
   A: Adam
   B: Andrew
   C: Isaac
   D: David

8. One of the most famous humanoid robots is *Star Trek: The Next Generation*'s Data, played by Brent Spiner. But in which movie does Data die?
   A: *Star Trek VI: The Undiscovered Country (1991)*
   B: *Star Trek Generations (1994)*
   C: *Star Trek: First Contact (1996)*
   D: *Star Trek: Nemesis (2002)*

9. In *Ex Machina (2014)*, what test is the robotic Ava subjected to at the start of the film?

10. In *Blade Runner* and *Blade Runner 2049 (2017)*, what test do replicants undergo to tell them apart from humans?

HUMANOID ROBOTS

1. The 'Maschinenmensch' in Fritz Lang's *Metropolis (1927)* is one of the most iconic robots in movie history. But what is the name of the human character whose appearance it emulates?

    A: Maria

    B: Mary

    C: Monica

    D: Margaret

2. What was the eponymous theme park in the sequel to *Westworld (1973)*?

3. *RoboCop (1987)* is the most famous robotic cop, despite technically being a cyborg. The cyborg was created by the evil, anagrammatic corporation, OCP. But what does its name stand for?

4. By the time of *Ghost in the Shell (1995)*, cybernetic crime fighters are commonplace. But what year is the film set in?

    A: 1999

    B: 2014

    C: 2029

    D: 2050

5. In *Austin Powers: International Man of Mystery (1997)*, the feminine robots that attack Austin Powers are:

    A: Gynoids

    B: Fembots

    C: Robotesses

    D: GirlTrons

6. *Astro Boy (2009)* is a robotic recreation of Toby Tenma. But who wrote the *Astro Boy* manga that the movie was based on?

7. Who played RoboCop in the 2014 remake of the film?

8. Why don't we see the face of the cyborg protagonist of *Hardcore Henry (2015)*?

9. *A.I. Artificial Intelligence (2001)* was directed by Steven Spielberg, but which famous director originally acquired the rights to the story?

10. In the film *T.I.M. (2023)* what does T.I.M.'s name stand for?

    A: Tactile Intelligence Mainframe

    B: Tachyon Interface Manifest

    C: Timed Informational Mechanism

    D: Technologically Integrated Manservant

HUMANOID ROBOTS

1. The short silent film *A Clever Dummy (1917)* features a mechanical automaton that resembles a man, but why isn't it referred to as a robot?

2. In *The Perfect Woman (1949)*, what is the one word that must never be said in front of the female robot, 'Olga'?

3. In *The Colossus of New York (1958)*, Dr William Spensser transplants his son's brain into a robotic body so that he can continue his work. What work is that?

4. What is the Data-Analyzing Robot Youth Lifeform (D.A.R.Y.L.) originally designed as in the movie, *D.A.R.Y.L. (1985)*?

5. In *Terminator 2: Judgment Day (1991)*, John Connor is pursued by the deadly liquid metal T-2000, but what sort of Terminator does Arnold Schwarzenegger play in that film?

6. Which Brian Aldiss short story is *A.I. Artificial Intelligence (2001)* based on?

7. While there are a lot of films about men using robotics to build the perfect woman, the German film *I'm Your Man (2021)* is one of the few films where a woman is introduced to her ideal robotic man. Who directed this film?

8. In *After Yang (2021)*, the young girl, Mika, is bought a robotic brother, Yang, to help her connect with her Chinese heritage. Who plays her adoptive father?

9. Which high-tech toy company does Cady's aunt, Gemma, work for in *M3GAN (2022)*?

10. In *Brian and Charles (2022)*, how does Brian Gittins' homemade robot companion learn English?

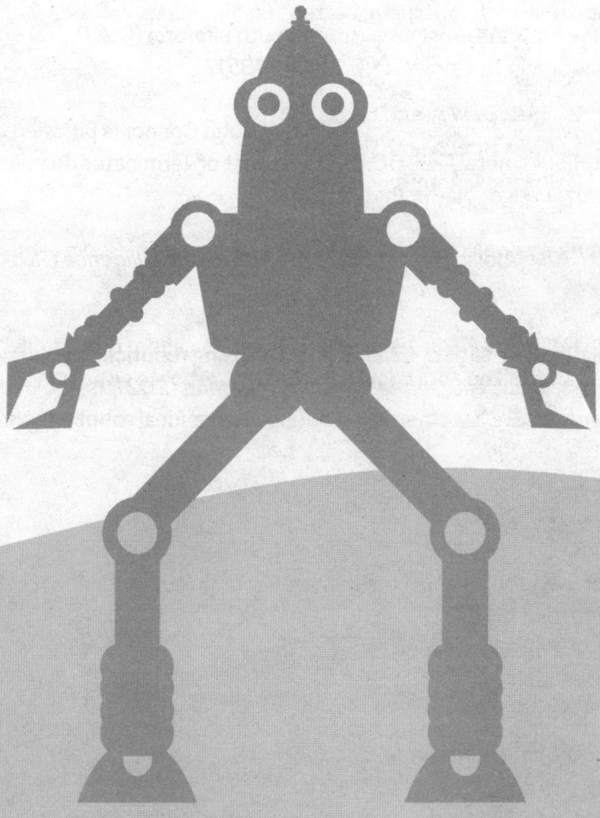

NON-HUMANOID ROBOTS

Human bodies are great and all, but they go wrong all the time. Why limit yourself to that when you can make a robot look like literally anything? Even a metal box on wheels with some flashing LEDs on top!

1. Which body part was the Tin Man missing in *The Wizard of Oz (1939)*?
   A: His brain
   B: His heart
   C: His courage

2. What names did Lowell give his robot companions in *Silent Running (1972)*?
   A: Moe, Larry and Curly
   B: Huey, Dewey and Louie
   C: Alvin, Simon and Theodore
   D: Porthos, Aramis and Athos

3. What name does robot Number Five give himself in *Short Circuit (1986)*?

4. While *RoboCop (1987)* is best known for its cyborg protagonist, what is the name of the actual law enforcement robot to appear in the film?
   A: CP-504
   B: R3-K19
   C: TX-118
   D: ED-209

5. Which weapon disables the human-hunting 'Sentinel' robots in *The Matrix (1999)*?
   A: Nuclear weapon
   B: Tesla coils
   C: EMP
   D: Water cannon

6. Which hero does the titular robot in *The Iron Giant* want to be like?
    - A: Iron Man
    - B: Superman
    - C: Batman
    - D: Spider-Man

7. In *Wild Wild West (1999),* Will Smith and Kevin Kline must fight what kind of robotic animal?
    - A: A spider
    - B: A scorpion
    - C: A lobster
    - D: A crab

8. In *Stealth (2005)*, the heroes must track down an AI that has been equipped to which piece of military equipment?

9. In *Chappie (2015),* the law enforcement robot is built by the weapons company Tetravaal. Which actor plays the CEO of the company?
    - A: Brian Cox
    - B: Sigourney Weaver
    - C: Sam Rockwell
    - D: Tilda Swinton

10. In *Finch (2021)*, the protagonist is trying to build a robot to do what job?
    - A: Keep him company
    - B: Look after his dog
    - C: Salvage supplies
    - D: Alert him to threats

NON-HUMANOID ROBOTS

1. In the silent film *The Master Mystery (1918)*, a company steals an inventor's design for a powerful automaton. They are investigated by Justice Department agent Quentin Locke, who was played by which famous magician?

2. *The Mechanical Man (1921)* is thought to be the first film to depict robot-on-robot violence. What country was it made in?
    - A: Belgium
    - B: Italy
    - C: France
    - D: Spain

3. *The Mechanical Monsters (1941)* sees an army of giant robots fight which popular hero?

4. In *Logan's Run (1976)*, what is the name of the robot that stops Runners escaping the city?
    - A: Box
    - B: Tank
    - C: Guardian
    - D: Logan

5. Which was the second killer robot movie Michael Crichton directed?
    - A: *Short Circuit*
    - B: *Terminator*
    - C: *Runaway*
    - D: *Bladerunner*

6. What is the name of the robot that caused the shuttle launch in *SpaceCamp (1986)*?

    A: Lucky

    B: Glitch

    C: Gremlin

    D: Jinx

7. According to the title of the 1987 movie directed by Matthew Robins, what do its robotic flying saucers not include?

8. In *Robot & Frank (2012)*, what is the first thing the robot helps Frank steal?

9. In *Interstellar (2014)*, how honest is the robot TARS when Cooper first meets him?

10. In the Korean space flick, *Space Sweepers (2021)*, what is Robot Bubs saving up for?

    A: A new voice

    B: An extra robot arm

    C: A skin graft

    D: A 'Free Will' chip

NON-HUMANOID ROBOTS

1. *The Automatic Motorist (1911)* is one of the earliest examples of a robotically driven car, but it is a remake of which film?

2. In the 1940 serial *Mysterious Doctor Satan*, the evil Doctor Satan plans to unleash a robotic army on the world with only the mysterious 'Copperhead' standing in his way. What is Copperhead's secret identity?

3. What was the name of the robot monster in the movie *Robot Monster (1953)*?

4. *Forbidden Planet*'s *(1956)* Robby the Robot is one of the most famous robots in cinema history, and has cameoed in numerous TV shows - name one other *film* he has appeared in.

5. Which esteemed literary author wrote the screenplay for the Kirk Douglas-starring killer robot movie, *Saturn 3 (1980)*?

6. Despite being set in ancient times, the movie *Clash of the Titans (1981)* features Bubo, a robotic sidekick who resembles which animal?

7. The Protector 101 series security robots murder a shopping centre full of teenagers in which horror film?

8. In the movie *Screamers (1995)*, Colonel Hendricksson has to cross a battlefield patrolled by robotic weapons he helped create. But which famous cyborg actor plays Hendricksson?
9. What is the name of the robot in the 1998 movie, *Lost in Space*?
10. Robot boxing movie *Real Steel (2011)* is (very) loosely based on which short story?

SUPERCOMPUTERS!

In this day and age, maybe the whole idea of robots is old hat. After all, why bother crushing someone with your mighty metal arms when you can just drain their bank account, launch their nuclear weapons, or open all the airlocks on their spaceship?

1. In *2001: A Space Odyssey (1968)*, what song does the HAL 9000 computer sing as it is shut down?
   A: 'Waltzing Matilda'
   B: 'The Sun Has Got His Hat On'
   C: 'Daisy Bell'
   D: 'Twinkle, Twinkle, Little Star'

2. In the John Carpenter movie, *Dark Star (1974)*, what artificially intelligent device must Doolittle debate to save the ship?
   A: A bomb
   B: The navigation computer
   C: A door
   D: A medical bot

3. Which space probe is the true identity of the artificial intelligence that approaches Earth in *Star Trek: The Motion Picture (1979)*?
   A: Voyager 2
   B: Voyager 6
   C: Pioneer 10
   D: Pioneer 11

4. In *WarGames (1983)*, what game does David Lightman instruct the WOPR to play to prevent it from starting a nuclear war?
   A: Tic-Tac-Toe
   B: Go
   C: Chess
   D: Backgammon

5. What is the name of the U.S. Robotics supercomputer in *I, Robot (2004)*?
   A: VIKI
   B: BEKI
   C: HANA
   D: ELLA

6. What answer does the computer in *The Hitchhiker's Guide to the Galaxy (2005)* provide to 'Life, the universe and everything'?

7. Aside from talking, how does Sam Bell's AI companion GERTY communicate with him in *Moon (2009)*?
   A: Writing
   B: Playing songs
   C: Emojis
   D: Photographs

8. Who wrote and directed the AI romance movie *Her (2013)*?

9. In *Big Bug (2022)* why do the household robots trap their family inside the house?

10. What is the name of the AI antagonist of *Mission Impossible: Dead Reckoning Part One (2023)*?
    A: The Intelligence
    B: The Entity
    C: Overseer
    D: Oracle

SUPERCOMPUTERS!

1. Who provided HAL 9000's voice in *2001: A Space Odyssey (1968)* and *2010: The Year We Make Contact (1984)*?

2. In *Colossus: The Forbin Project (1970)* 'Colossus' is the name of the US military's advanced supercomputer. What is the USSR's supercomputer called?
    A: Guardian
    B: Citadel
    C: Bastion
    D: Vigilance

3. Which very low number is the name of the computer that holds all human knowledge in *Rollerball (1975)*?

4. In *Demon Seed (1977)*, why does the Proteus IV AI program want to capture Susan?
    A: To harvest her for parts
    B: To implant its mind in her brain
    C: To impregnate her
    D: To dissect her

5. In *WarGames (1983)*, what does WOPR stand for?

6. What was the name of Steve Barron's directorial debut about a man and woman caught in a love triangle with a sentient PC?

7. In *Terminator 2: Judgment Day (1991)*, who is responsible for creating Skynet?
    A: Freeman Dyson
    B: Miles Dyson
    C: James Dyson
    D: George Dyson

8. In *Moon (2009)*, what does the sign say on the back of GERTY's monitor?

    A: I'm with stupid!

    B: My other computer's an Apple Mac

    C: Kick me

    D: Out of order

9. In *Transcendence (2014)*, what is the name of the terrorist organisation targeting AI laboratories?

    A: Robotic Insurrection From Tyranny

    B: Radical Individual Free Thought

    C: Real Intelligence Freedom Taskforce

    D: Revolutionary Independence From Technology

10. In *Superintelligence (2020)*, why does the AI make contact with Carol Peters?

    A: To judge humanity

    B: To ask her to rescue it

    C: To learn what love is

    D: To warn her of a disaster

SUPERCOMPUTERS!

1. In *2010: The Year We Make Contact (1984)*, what is the name of the feminine version of Hal 9000?

2. Who directed *Colossus: The Forbin Project (1970)*?

3. What philosophical concept does Doolittle use to debate the AI in *Dark Star (1974)*?

4. The AI horror movie *Demon Seed (1977)* is based on a book by which famous horror novelist?

5. What is the name of the computer that controls the futuristic prison in *Fortress (1992)*?

6. In *The Hitchhiker's Guide to the Galaxy (2005)*, what is the name of the most powerful computer ever built?

7. What is the name of Theodore's AI assistant in *Her (2013)*?

8. In the killer artificial intelligence movie *Singularity (2017)*, which actor was added to the film through new footage four years after its original 2013 release?

9. The movie *Tau (2018)* is named after the AI that runs the house its abducted protagonists are trapped in. But what is the name of the killer robot inside the house?

10. In *Superintelligence (2020)*, which celebrity does the AI imitate to put the protagonist, Carol, at ease?

MONSTERS AND MUTANTS

Environmental organisations estimate that between 10,000 and 100,000 species go extinct every year. But how many new ones are evolving? How many linger, still undiscovered on some ancient island or in the deepest underwater crevice? And how many, even now, are growing in some unsuspecting petri dish in some classified government laboratory?

PREHISTORIC BEASTS

A lot of science fiction talks about humans being the most dangerous animal, because of our ability to think, build tools and work together. But some science fiction talks about the animals that ruled the Earth before humans, who were dangerous because they were massive and had really sharp teeth.

1. The pioneering dinosaur movie, *The Lost World (1925)* is based on a book by which author?
   A: Arthur Conan Doyle
   B: Jules Verne
   C: Michael Crichton
   D: Robert J. Saywer

2. Which island does King Kong live on?
   A: Isla Nublar
   B: Isla de Muerta
   C: Skull Island
   D: Skeleton Island

3. Where does the eponymous beast from *The Beast from 20,000 Fathoms (1953)* come from?
   A: It thaws out of the ice
   B: It swims out of the Mariana Trench
   C: It is awoken by an underwater volcano
   D: It escaped from an underwater laboratory

4. Which vehicle is used to travel to the subcontinent Caprona in *The Land That Time Forgot (1974)*?
   A: A hot air balloon
   B: An aeroplane
   C: A German U-boat
   D: An airship

5. What is the name of the island the park is built on in *Jurassic Park (1993)*?

6. In *A Sound of Thunder (2005)*, the time-travellers visit the prehistoric age to hunt which dinosaur?

A: A Tyrannosaurus rex
B: An Allosaurus
C: A Velociraptor
D: A Stegosaurus

7. In *Journey to the Center of the Earth (2008)*, who does Trevor Anderson go to the centre of the Earth looking for?

8. What is the name of the reptilian humanoids that live in *The Land of the Lost (2009)*?

A: Sleestacks
B: Aquaphibians
C: Homo Reptilia
D: Silurians

9. In *The Meg (2018)*, which action star faces off against the giant prehistoric shark?

10. Which dinosaur-infested planet does Adam Driver's character land on in *65 (2023)*?

PREHISTORIC BEASTS

1. What is the name of the ship in the 1933 and 2005 versions of *King Kong*?
   - A: S.S. *Narcissus*
   - B: S.S. *Victory*
   - C: S.S. *Pioneer*
   - D: S.S. *Venture*

2. What sort of fictional dinosaur is the creature in *The Beast From 20,000 Fathoms (1953)*?
   - A: Plesiosaur
   - B: Aquasaurus
   - C: Rhedosaurus
   - D: Rosasaurus

3. Who created the pioneering dinosaur effects for *The Lost World (1925)*?
   - A: Ray Harryhausen
   - B: Willis O'Brien
   - C: Nick Park
   - D: Norman McLaren

4. While trekking across Jurassic Park in the film of the same name, Grant, Lex and Tim have to hide from a stampede of which running dinosaur?

5. Which low-budget 90s dinosaur movie was licensed for the 2022 video game, *High on Life*?

6. Dinosaurs escaped extinction by moving to a parallel universe in which 90s video game-to-film adaptation?

7. Of these characters in Peter Jackson's *King Kong (2005)*, which was *not* in the original 1933 film?
    A: Jack Driscoll
    B: Carl Denham
    C: Bruce Baxter
    D: Ann Darrow

8. In *The Land of the Lost (2009)*, what science did Dr Rick Marshall found?

9. In *The Meg (2018)* what is 'Meg' short for?
    A: Megalodon
    B: Megalosaurus
    C: Megadopterus
    D: Megatherium

10. As well as *65 (2023)*, the writing duo of Scott Beck and Adam Woods co-wrote which other monster movie?

PREHISTORIC BEASTS

1. Before *The Lost World (1925)*, Willis O'Brien made stop-motion dinosaurs for which 1918 film?

2. Which of these classic dinosaur films had stop-motion dinosaurs *not* made by Ray Harryhausen?
   A: *The Valley of the Gwangi (1969)*
   B: *The Giant Behemoth (1959)*
   C: *One Million Years B.C. (1966)*

3. Name one of the directors of the original 1933 *King Kong* movie.

4. At the climax of *The Beast from 20,000 Fathoms (1953)*, how does Dr Nesbitt get high enough to shoot the Beast's eye?

5. What was the sequel to *The Land That Time Forgot (1974)* called?

6. John Goodman supplied the voice of a Tyrannosaurus rex in which movie?

7. Of the actors who appeared in the original *Jurassic Park (1993)*, who has appeared in the most sequels?

8. Which actor had to be sued to play the human partner of a dinosaur detective in *Theodore Rex (1996)*?

9. In Peter Jackson's 2005 *King Kong* remake, a crate is seen containing what creature from his previous movies?

10. What is the name of Adam Driver's character in *65 (2023)*?

MUTATIONS AND CREATIONS

People who say scientists shouldn't play God underestimate just how much fun it is to play. Whether you are sticking a bunch of DNA in a blender, stitching some body parts together and electrocuting them, or simply nuking areas full of wildlife to see what crawls out, movie scientists have created a wondrous menagerie.

1. Who played the original monster-created-by-science in *Frankenstein (1931)*?

2. When the original *Godzilla (1954)* was released in the USA it was re-edited for American audiences. What title was it released under?
   A: *Godzilla Attacks!*
   B: *Godzilla, King of the Monsters!*
   C: *Godzilla*
   D: *Godzilla Vs Tokyo*

3. In the 1954 movie, *Them!*, which creatures grow to a gigantic size as a result of atomic testing?
   A: Spiders
   B: Termites
   C: Ants
   D: Cockroaches

4. In the 1996 adaptation of H.G. Wells' *The Island of Doctor Moreau*, who plays the titular doctor?
   A: Christopher Lloyd
   B: Tom Baker
   C: Marlon Brando
   D: Leonard Nimoy

5. Which famously monster-obsessed director created the 1997 killer-bug film, *Mimic*?

6. Which actor is famously eaten by genetically modified sharks after delivering a heroic speech in *Deep Blue Sea (1999)*?

7. The monster in the Korean movie, *The Host (2006)* is created because which chemical is dumped in the Han River?

    A: Radioactive waste

    B: Formaldehyde

    C: Dichloro-diphenyl-trichloroethane

    D: Sulphuric acid

8. What name is given to the animal-human hybrid in *Splice (2009)*?

    A: Dani

    B: Donna

    C: Deb

    D: Dren

9. *Journey 2: The Mysterious Island (2012)* features a journey to an island teeming with genetically modified life, but it was filmed as a sequel to which other Jules Verne novel?

10. Who stars in the genetically modified giant animal movie *Rampage (2018)*?

    A: Dwayne 'The Rock' Johnson

    B: Vin Diesel

    C: John Cena

    D: Chris Evans

11. Can you name all of the turtles in *Teenage Mutant Ninja Turtles: Mutant Mayhem (2023)*?

MUTATIONS AND CREATIONS

1. When was the first screen adaptation of Mary Shelley's *Frankenstein* released?

    A: 1910

    B: 1924

    C: 1931

    D: 1945

2. In *Godzilla (1954)* what is the name of the first ship destroyed by Godzilla?

    A: *Kobayashi Maru*

    B: *Hakudo Maru*

    C: *Nippon Maru*

    D: *Elko Maru*

3. *The Mysterious Island (1961)* features giant birds, bees and even ammonites. Which famous submariner is behind their creation?

4. In the 1977 adaptation of *The Island of Doctor Moreau*, what do the human-animal hybrids call Doctor Moreau's laboratory?

    A: The Monster Factory

    B: The House of Pain

    C: The Temple of Creation

    D: The Genesis Chamber

5. The monsters in *Mimic (1997)* are genetically engineered hybrids of which two insects?

6. Which kind of sharks do they genetically modify in *Deep Blue Sea (1999)*?

    A: Great Whites

    B: Hammerheads

    C: Makos

    D: Tiger

7. The director of *The Host (2006)*, Bong Joon-ho, won a Best Picture Oscar for a film with a thematically linked name to his earlier monster movie. What was it?

8. Who played Clive Nicoli in *Splice (2009)*?

9. What was *Rampage (2018)* based on?

10. In what year was the first Teenage Mutant Ninja Turtles movie released?

MUTATIONS AND CREATIONS

1. In *Frankenstein (1931)* and its sequel, *Bride of Frankenstein (1935)*, what is Dr Frankenstein's first name?

2. What is the name of the first movie adaptation of *The Island of Doctor Moreau*?

3. Who directed *Godzilla (1954)*?

4. In *The Mysterious Island (1961)*, the protagonists are soldiers from which historic war?

5. *Empire of the Ants (1977)*, which sees ants mutated by radioactive waste, is an adaptation of a story by which writer?

6. What nickname is given to the monster in *Mimic (1997)*?

7. In *Deep Blue Sea (1999)*, scientists genetically engineer sharks with bigger brains to find a cure for which disease?

8. Bong Joon-ho's 2017 movie, *Okja*, features what genetically modified animal?

9. Before creating a human-animal hybrid, the scientists in *Splice (2009)* create two other genetically engineered creatures. What are they called?

10. In *Poor Things (2023)*, what is the name of Willem Dafoe's mad scientist character?

NEW SPECIES

Not everything is a living fossil or a scientific abomination. Much of the natural world is yet to be discovered. But when you encounter a species previously unknown to science, you have to ask: 'Has nobody ever seen this animal before... or has nobody ever seen this animal before and survived?'

1. To play the *Creature from the Black Lagoon (1954),* Ricou Browning had to perform underwater without breathing apparatus for long periods. According to his daughter, how long could he hold his breath?

    A: Three minutes

    B: Four minutes

    C: Five minutes

    D: Six minutes

2. In *Monster from the Ocean Floor (1954)*, what is the monster?

    A: A giant amoeba

    B: A giant octopus

    C: A plesiosaur

    D: A sea serpent

3. In *It Came from Beneath the Sea (1955),* a giant monster attacks which famous landmark?

    A: The Statue of Liberty

    B: The White House

    C: The Golden Gate Bridge

    D: Alcatraz

4. In the movie *Gremlins (1984),* what name does Randall Peltzer give the Mogwai?

5. Which killer spider movie is named after a fear of spiders?

6. Who plays Valentine 'Val' McKee in the underground monster movie, *Tremors (1990)*?
   - A: Bruce Campbell
   - B: Kevin Bacon
   - C: Dennis Quaid
   - D: Bill Pullman

7. In *Gremlins 2: The New Batch (1990)*, how does Billy eventually kill the Gremlins?
   - A: Sunlight
   - B: Electricity
   - C: Fire
   - D: Water

8. In *Cloverfield (2008)*, what are the characters celebrating before the monster turns up?
   - A: A farewell party
   - B: A stag party
   - C: A birthday party
   - D: A New Year's Eve party

9. Name three of the monsters on the board in *The Cabin in the Woods' (2011)* sweepstake.

10. In *Underwater (2020)*, the Kepler 822 base is at the bottom of which famous oceanic trench?

NEW SPECIES

1. What was special about the way *Creature from the Black Lagoon (1954)* was shown in theatres?
2. *Monster from the Ocean Floor (1954)* was the first film produced by which cult Hollywood legend known as 'The Pope of Pop Cinema'?
3. What technique is used to simulate the giant octopus in *It Came from Beneath the Sea (1954)*?
4. In *Gremlins (1984)*, what rules must you obey in taking care of a Mogwai?
5. What container is the Venezuelan spider in *Arachnophobia (1990)* transported to the US in?

   A: A box of fruit
   B: A passenger's shoes
   C: A sample box
   D: A coffin

6. What name is given to the wormlike creatures that attack the town of Perfection in *Tremors (1990)*?

   A: Sandworms
   B: Graboids
   C: Snatchers
   D: Tremorites

7. *Gremlins 2: The New Batch (1990)* takes place in a tower block owned by which fictional billionaire?

8. In *Cloverfield (2008)*, what is the nickname of the character holding the camera for most of the film?

9. Who plays 'The Director' in *The Cabin in the Woods (2011)*?
   - A: Joss Whedon
   - B: Gary Oldman
   - C: Sigourney Weaver
   - D: Cate Blanchett

10. In the Guillermo Del Toro film, *The Shape of Water (2017)*, Doug Jones plays an amphibious humanoid who falls in love with a human. What is the name of the other amphibious humanoid Doug Jones has played in a Guillermo Del Toro film?

NEW SPECIES

1. In *Creature from the Black Lagoon (1954)* the Black Lagoon itself is in which rainforest?

2. What vehicle is used to hunt the *Monster from the Ocean Floor (1954)*?

3. How many legs does the giant octopus in *It Came From Beneath the Sea (1954)* have?

4. What small town is *Gremlins (1984)* primarily set in?

5. When an entomologist first examines one of the Venezuelan spiders from *Arachnophobia (1990)*, what does he notice about it?

6. How do the monsters in *Tremors (1990)* detect their prey?

7. In *Gremlins 2: The New Batch (1990)*, how does the 'Brain Gremlin' make a gremlin immune to sunlight?

8. What critical clue can be seen in the background of the final scene of *Cloverfield (2008)*?

9. In *The Cabin in the Woods (2011),* name four of the archetypes which *must* be sacrificed for the ritual to succeed.

10. In *The Shape of Water (2011)*, the amphibian humanoid is kept captive at what facility?

FIRST CONTACT

Does intelligent life exist out there in the universe? Is it truly possible that in the infinite cosmos, only one world has been gifted the spark of sapience? On distant planets, do minds exist with the knowledge to examine the world around them, sharing stories and ideas and a willingness to comprehend other perspectives?

WE COME IN PEACE

The second-best-case scenario for first contact is that aliens who are smarter and better people than us will come to our planet and finally get us to stop polluting everywhere and warring with each other all the time. The best-case scenario is that, with junk food and pop culture, we can make them as bad as us.

1. What name does the alien Klaatu assume to move among humans in *The Day the Earth Stood Still (1951)*?

   A: John Smith

   B: John Doe

   C: Mr Carpenter

   D: Ford Prefect

2. In *The Man Who Fell to Earth (1976)*, the alien Thomas Jerome Newton is played by which otherworldly singer?

3. Who directed *Close Encounters of the Third Kind (1977)*?

   A: Steven Spielberg

   B: George Lucas

   C: Peter Jackson

   D: Richard Donner

4. What does E.T. stand for?

5. In John Carpenter's *Starman (1984)*, an alien comes to visit Earth after finding which space probe?

   A: Voyager 2

   B: Pioneer 10

   C: Viking 1

   D: Galileo

6. What name does David give the robotic alien spaceship commander in *Flight of the Navigator (1986)*?

   A: Al

   B: Sam

   C: Max

   D: Bob

7. The widely panned *E.T.* imitator *Mac and Me (1988)*, famously features prominent product placement for which fast food restaurant?

8. *Contact (1997)* is based on a novel by which famous American astronomer?

A: Gregory Benford
B: Carl Sagan
C: David Brin
D: Fred Hoyle

9. What country is the alien internment camp, *District 9 (2009)* based in?

A: South Africa
B: Uganda
C: Kenya
D: Nigeria

10. Who voices the stoner alien visitor in *Paul (2011)*?

A: Seth Rogen
B: Jack Black
C: Jeff Bridges
D: Zach Galifianakis

11. The aliens in *Arrival (2016)* are named after which comedy duo?

A: Laurel and Hardy
B: Morecambe and Wise
C: Abbott and Costello
D: Hale and Pace

WE COME IN PEACE

1. In *The Day the Earth Stood Still (1951)*, how does Klaatu demonstrate his power to the human race?

2. In *The Man Who Fell to Earth (1976)*, Thomas Jerome Newton comes to Earth seeking out what resource?

    A: Oil
    B: Water
    C: Gold
    D: Oxygen

3. In *Close Encounters of the Third Kind (1977)*, the aliens' subliminal messaging provokes Roy Neary to make a model of the Devils Tower in Wyoming out of which foodstuff?

4. With which food does Elliot lure the eponymous alien into his house in *E.T. The Extra-Terrestrial (1982)*?

    A: Smarties
    B: M&Ms
    C: Reese's Pieces
    D: Jelly Babies

5. In *Starman (1984)*, whose human form does the alien assume?

6. What planet does the alien in *Flight of the Navigator (1986)* come from?

    A: Phaeton
    B: Phaelon
    C: Photon
    D: Phaeron

7. In *Mac and Me (1988)*, what does 'MAC' stand for?

8. In *Contact (1997)*, the alien signal Dr Arroway detects is revealed to be footage of what person?

9. What derogatory slur is used to refer to the aliens in *District 9 (2009)*?

10. In *Paul (2011)*, the alien Paul persuades Ruth Buggs to question her beliefs by curing which body part?
    - A: Her hand
    - B: Her eye
    - C: Her legs
    - D: Her head

11. In *Arrival (2016)*, China attempts to communicate with the aliens by playing what game with them?

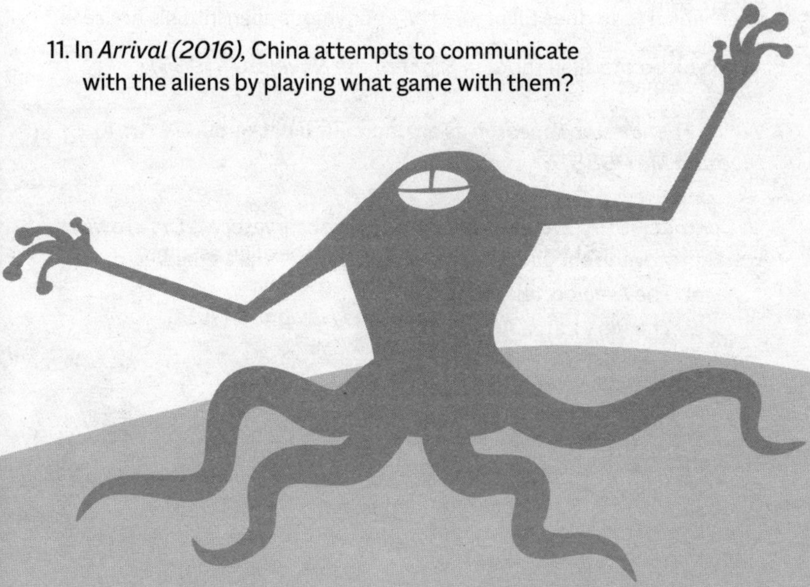

WE COME IN PEACE

1. In *The Day the Earth Stood Still (1951)*, Klaatu urges Helen Benson to remember the command 'Klaatu barada nikto'. This phrase is later used as a magic spell in which zombie movie?

2. Who wrote the book that *The Man Who Fell to Earth (1976)* is based on?

3. *Close Encounters of the Third Kind (1964)* was the second film Steven Spielberg made about aliens. He made his first when he was 17. What was it called?

4. What flower does *E.T.* revive?

5. According to the alien in *Starman (1984)*, what does the yellow traffic light mean?

6. Who voiced the alien robot in *Flight of the Navigator (1986)*?

7. Which *Friends* star appeared as an uncredited background extra in *Mac and Me (1988)*?

8. In *Contact (1997)*, which radio astronomy observatory is Dr Arroway working at when she first detects an extraterrestrial signal?
   A: The Arecibo Telescope
   B: The Very Large Array
   C: Jodrell Bank

9. What weapons manufacturer oversees the alien internment camp in *District 9 (2009)*?

10. What famous TV robot do Clive and Graeme see at San Diego Comic-Con in *Paul (2011)*?

11. As a result of her experiences in *Arrival (2016)*, Louise Banks writes a book about the alien hectapod language. What is it called?

CLOSE ENCOUNTERS OF THE SCARY KIND

The thing about encountering alien intelligence is that there is a real gulf of understanding. We are so shaped by our environment that even the most basic forms of communication might not translate between planets. What we're saying is, are these aliens trying to turn you inside out, lay their eggs in you and drink your brains out through a straw? Or is that just their way of saying 'Hello'?

1. Where is the research base located in *The Thing from Another World (1951)*?

    A: The Arctic

    B: The Antarctic

2. In *The Quatermass Xperiment (1955)*, what is Quatermass' first name?

    A: Brendan

    B: Bernard

    C: Barnaby

    D: Bartholemew

3. In *The Blob (1958)*, who plays Steve Andrews?

    A: Marlon Brando

    B: James Dean

    C: Charlton Heston

    D: Steve McQueen

4. In *The Andromeda Strain (1971)*, what is the name of the secret government facility?

    A: Wildfire

    B: Torchwood

    C: Inferno

    D: Beacon

5. In the 1982 movie, what form does *The Thing* assume when the characters first meet it?

6. The design of the alien hybrid in *Species (1995)* is the work of which famous alien designer?

7. Who stars as the alien protagonist of *Under the Skin (2013)*?
    A: Olivia Wilde
    B: Eva Green
    C: Scarlett Johansson
    D: Gemma Arterton

8. In *Sputnik (2020)*, the extraterrestrial life form becomes visible when its cosmonaut host does what?

9. In *Significant Other (2022)*, which of the film's protagonist couple is replaced by an alien imposter?
    A: Ruth
    B: Harry

10. Which name does OJ give to the predatory UFO in *Nope (2022)*?
    A: Jean Jacket
    B: Red Rum
    C: Hurricane Fly
    D: Man o' War

CLOSE ENCOUNTERS OF THE SCARY KIND

1. *The Thing from Another World (1951)* and *The Thing (1982)* are both based on which short story?

2. In *The Quatermass Xperiment (1955)*, what organisation launches the first manned rocket into outer space?

3. At the end of *The Blob (1958)*, the titular Blob is frozen and transported to the Arctic. How long does Dave Barton predict this will stop the Blob?

4. In *The Andromeda Strain* (1971), why is Dr Hall entrusted with the key to deactivate the facility's self-destruct mechanism?
   - A: Because he is the oldest
   - B: Because he is the youngest
   - C: Because he is unmarried
   - D: Because he has no children

5. In *The Thing (1982)*, what do the characters apply to blood samples to tell if they are from a human?
   - A: Extreme heat
   - B: Water
   - C: Litmus paper
   - D: Acid

6. Why do the scientists in *Species (1995)* choose to make the alien-human hybrid female?

7. In *Men in Black (1997)* what is the name of the farmer the bug wears as a skinsuit?
    - A: Clyde
    - B: Doug
    - C: Edgar
    - D: Ronald

8. Which city does the protagonist of *Under the Skin (2013)* patrol looking for victims?

9. Jamie Lee Curtis starred in which 1999 film about a salvage crew that discovers a ship overtaken by an alien entity?

10. In *Significant Other (2022)*, the alien imposter is forced to fight what sea creature?

11. What must you avoid doing to prevent the killer UFO in *Nope (2022)* from attacking you?

CLOSE ENCOUNTERS OF THE SCARY KIND

1. How is the creature in *The Thing From Another World (1951)* eventually killed?

2. Who wrote the serial that *The Quatermass Xperiment (1955)* was based on?

3. When *The Blob (1958)* eats a cinema, what film is it showing?

4. In *The Andromeda Strain (1971)*, why is the baby immune to the alien microbe?

5. *The Thing (1982)* was nominated for a Razzie for its score by Ennio Morricone, but Morricone would later put unused music from that film in the Oscar-winning score to which Quentin Tarantino film?

6. Who is the main character and writer of the book that *Fire in the Sky (1993)* is based on?

7. As of 2024, how many sequels have been released to *Species (1995)*?

8. What food does the protagonist attempt to eat in *Under the Skin (2013)*?

9. What year is *Sputnik (2020)* set in?

10. In *Nope (2022),* OJ and Emerald's ancestor was a jockey in which historic piece of film footage?

ALIEN INVASION!

If we're lucky, maybe alien life won't want to eat our DNA or connect us to a galactic sense of cosmic oneness. Maybe they will just want to shoot us with guns and enslave the survivors.

1. In 1953, what was the first film to feature an invasion of aliens and their spacecraft in colour?

   A: *Invaders from Mars*

   B: *War of the Worlds*

   C: *It Came from Outer Space*

   D: *Target Earth*

2. In *Earth vs. the Flying Saucers (1956)*, what city do the aliens want to meet the world's leaders at?

   A: Geneva

   B: New York

   C: Washington D.C.

   D: Moscow

3. What are the aliens in *Invasion of the Body Snatchers (1956*) colloquially known as?

4. What must you wear to identify the alien infiltrators in *They Live (1988)*?

   A: Reading glasses

   B: 3D glasses

   C: Sunglasses

   D: X-ray specs

5. *Village of the Damned (1960)* is based on which John Wyndham novel?

   A: *The Chrysalids*

   B: *Trouble with Lichen*

   C: *The Midwich Cuckoos*

   D: *Chocky*

6. What is *Mars Attacks! (1996)* based on?
   A: A comic
   B: A TV show
   C: Trading cards
   D: A radio show

7. *The Faculty (1998)* stars which future Hobbit?
   A: Elijah Wood
   B: Sean Astin
   C: Dominic Monaghan
   D: Billy Boyd

8. Who starred as Ray Ferrier in the 2005 adaptation of *War of the Worlds*?
   A: Ben Affleck
   B: Matt Damon
   C: Tom Cruise
   D: Mark Wahlberg

9. *Attack the Block (2011)* features a nurse who would later play which alien?

10. How do the characters in *Grabbers (2012)* make themselves immune to the invading aliens?
    A: Getting angry
    B: Drinking alcohol
    C: Smoking cigarettes
    D: Not falling asleep

11. When Tom Cruise's character is infected with alien blood in *Edge of Tomorrow (2014)*, what effect does it have on him?

12. What are the aliens attracted to in *A Quiet Place (2018)*?
    A: Sound
    B: Light
    C: Heat
    D: Movement

ALIEN INVASION!

1. Who directed *Invaders from Mars (1953)*?
   - A: Jack Arnold
   - B: William Cameron Menzies
   - C: George Pal
   - D: Fred F. Sears

2. What kills the invaders in *The War of the Worlds (1953)*?
   - A: The common cold
   - B: Bacteria
   - C: The atom bomb
   - D: Air pollution

3. What is the name of the orbital satellite project in *Earth vs. the Flying Saucers (1956)*?

4. What town is invaded in *Invasion of the Body Snatchers (1956)*?

5. In *They Live (1988)* what two things is Roddy Piper's character here to do?

6. What physical features do the children born in *The Village of the Damned (1960)* share?

7. Who plays the President of the United States of America in *Mars Attacks! (1996)*?

8. What substance kills the infiltrating aliens in *The Faculty (1998)*?

9. Who narrates *War of the Worlds (2005)*?

10. On what night is *Attack the Block (2011)* set?

11. What is the name of the main family in *A Quiet Place (2018)*?

12. What are the aliens known as in *Captive State (2019)*?
    - A: Guardians
    - B: Overseers
    - C: Legislators
    - D: Judges

ALIEN INVASION!

1. *Invaders from Mars (1953)* was remade in 1986. Which famous sci-fi screenwriter worked on the script?

2. What is the name of the atomic scientist hero in *The War of the Worlds (1953)*?

3. What are the aliens' suits made out of in *Earth vs. the Flying Saucers (1956)*?

4. What is the name of the real-world delusion or syndrome in which a person believes a friend or family member has been replaced, as in *Invasion of the Body Snatchers*?

5. How are the aliens trying to make Earth like their home planet in *They Live (1988)*?

6. *Village of the Damned* was released in 1960, but it was remade again in what year?

7. In *Mars Attacks! (1996)* what animal's body is Sarah Jessica Parker's head stitched onto?

8. In the 2005 version of *War of the Worlds*, what is Tim Robbins' character's surname?

9. Which character in *Attack the Block (2011)* has Joe Cornish said was based on himself?

10. In *The World's End (2013)*, what name do Gary King and his friends give to the alien duplicates?

SPACE EXPLORATION

Of all the frontiers, space is definitely one of the last ones. Rather than waiting for aliens to come to us, let's get out into space ourselves. From the upper edges of Earth's atmosphere to the most distant boundaries of the universe itself, explorers are bound to encounter lots of new and exciting problems. But that won't stop us from bringing all our old ones along for good measure...

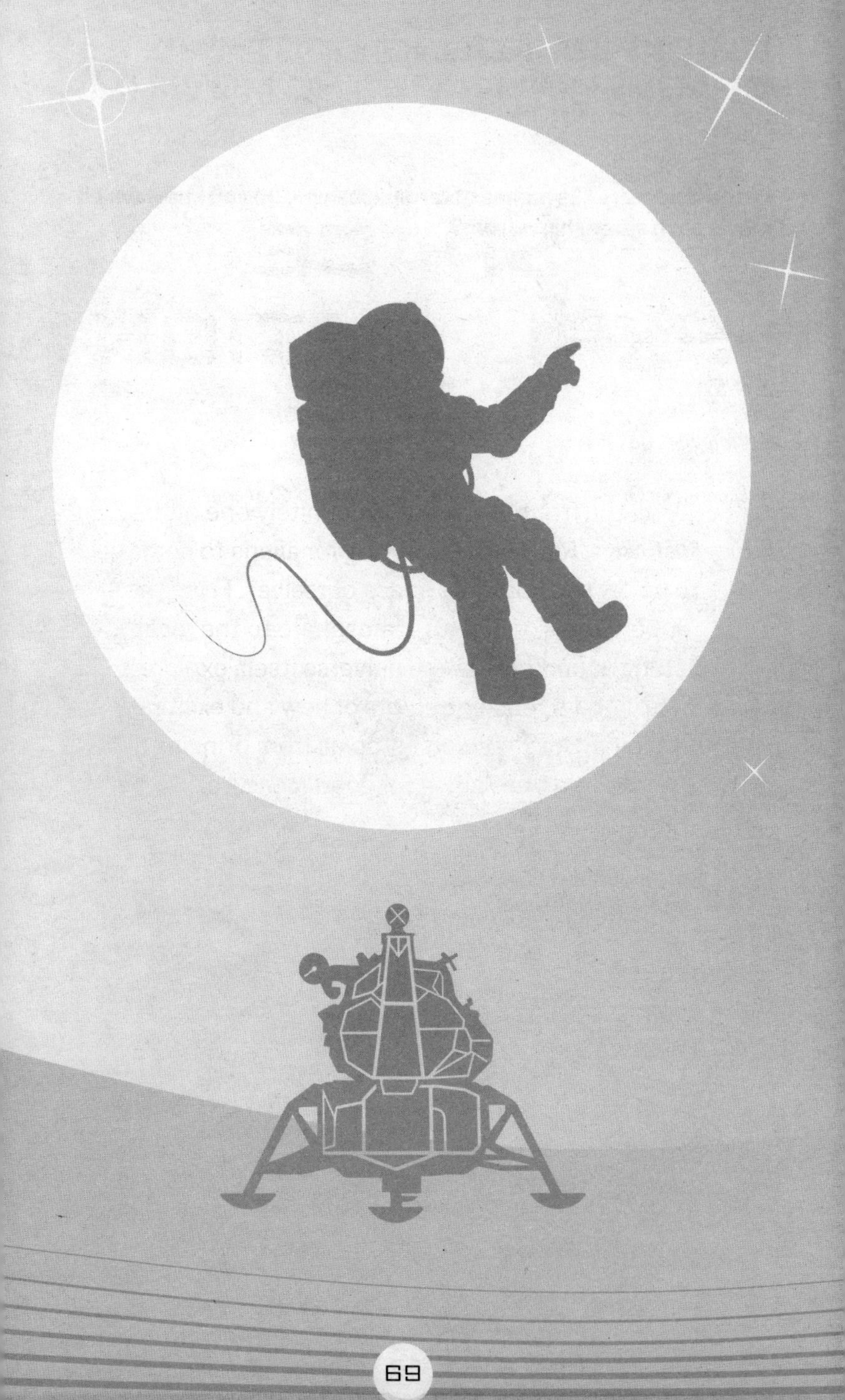

QUICKFIRE ROUND: SPOT THE SPACESHIP! NAME THE MOVIE!

Listed below are the names of ten spaceships. Do you know which movie each spaceship is from?

1. *Lewis & Clark*
2. *C-57D*
3. *Valley Forge*
4. *Discovery One*
5. *Heart of Gold*
6. *Endurance*
7. *Avalon*
8. *Icarus II*
9. *Hunter-Gratzner*
10. *Jupiter 2*

FROM EARTH TO THE MOON

If the universe is a swimming pool, this is the shallow end. Even after sixty years of manned spaceflight, we're still yet to venture outside of Earth's gravity well. But what's exciting is that even here we have still found many, many things that can go wrong.

1. *A Trip to the Moon (1902)* is one of the very earliest depictions of space travel in film. In the lunar mission it depicts, where does the space capsule hit the moon?

2. Which famous science fiction author contributed to the script of *Destination Moon* (1950)?

   A: Isaac Asimov
   B: Robert A. Heinlein
   C: Arthur C. Clarke
   D: Ray Bradbury

3. According to the movie *Forbidden Planet (1953)*, in what decade do humans first set foot on the moon?

   A: 1960s
   B: 1990s
   C: 2050s
   D: 2090s

4. What real-life type of spaceship do the astronauts get trapped on in *Marooned (1969)*?

   A: An Apollo module
   B: A Space Shuttle
   C: A Soyuz module
   D: A Mercury space capsule

5. Why do Wallace and Gromit decide to holiday on the moon in *A Grand Day Out (1989)*?

   A: Because everywhere else is booked up
   B: Because it has no rain
   C: Because it is made of cheese
   D: Because they couldn't think of anywhere else

6. What song does Sam Bell keep listening to in *Moon (2009)*?
   A: 'That's Amore' by Dean Martin and Deana Martin
   B: 'We Are the Champions' by Queen
   C: 'The One and Only' by Chesney Hawkes
   D: 'Man on the Moon' by R.E.M.

7. Gonzalo López-Gallego's first English-language film is a found-footage horror movie depicting which cancelled lunar mission?
   A: Apollo 16
   B: Apollo 17
   C: Apollo 18
   D: Apollo 19

8. Sandra Bullock's character is sent to upgrade which orbital structure in *Gravity (2013)*?
   A: International Space Station
   B: Mir
   C: Skylab
   D: The Hubble Telescope

9. What name is given to the increasingly hostile and dangerous lifeform captured in *Life (2017)*?
   A: Marvin
   B: Benji
   C: Calvin
   D: Digby

10. In the Korean movie *Space Sweepers (2021)*, the crew of the *Victory* find themselves in possession of a bomb disguised as what?

11. In *Moonfall (2022)*, what is the moon discovered to be?
   A: A megastructure
   B: A giant alien egg
   C: A black hole
   D: A spaceship

12. *I.S.S. (2024)* depicts what happens on the International Space Station during what event?
   A: World War 3
   B: An alien invasion
   C: An asteroid hitting the Earth
   D: A solar flare

FROM EARTH TO THE MOON

1. Who wrote, directed, produced and starred in *A Trip to the Moon (1902)*?

2. Which cartoon character stars in an informational video in *Destination Moon (1950)*?

    A: Woody Woodpecker
    B: Droopy Dog
    C: Bugs Bunny
    D: Porky Pig

3. In *Marooned (1969)*, who plays marooned astronaut 'Buzz' Lloyd?

4. Which famously space-age musical artist is the father of *Moon*'s director, Duncan Jones?

5. What payload is *Apollo 18 (2011)* sent to secretly deliver to the moon?

6. Which company does Max Da Costa work for in *Elysium (2013)*?

    A: Cyberdyne Corp
    B: Yoyodyne Corp
    C: Armadyne Corp
    D: Weynandyne Corp

7. In *Gravity (2013)*, what syndrome is the name of the debris cascade that kills Ryan Stone's crew?

8. Which book does Miranda North read towards the end of *Life (2017)*?

   A: *The Very Hungry Caterpillar*

   B: *The Little Prince*

   C: *Oh, The Places You'll Go!*

   D: *Goodnight Moon*

9. How is *Space Sweepers (2021)* a first for South Korea?

10. *Moonfall (2022)* is the second of Roland Emmerich's films to have 'Moon' in the title. Which is the first?

FROM EARTH TO THE MOON

1. In *A Trip to the Moon (1902)*, what name is given to the insectoid inhabitants of the moon?

2. Why don't the astronauts in *Destination Moon (1950)* have enough fuel to lift off the moon's surface?

3. What is the name of the fictional experimental spacecraft sent to rescue the astronauts in *Marooned (1969)*?

4. What substance is Sam Bell mining for in *Moon (2009)*?

5. What names are given to *Apollo 18*'s lander and command module?

6. In *Elysium (2013)*, the character of Julio is played by an actor who would go on to play another famous space resistance fighter. What's his name?

7. The voice of mission control in *Gravity (2013)* is provided by Ed Harris, who also ran NASA's mission control in which other movie?

8. Hiroyuki Sanada plays an astronaut in *Life (2017)*, but what was the first space movie he had a role in?

9. What does the Korean title of *Space Sweepers (2021)* translate as?

10. What kind of star is found to be at the centre of the moon in *Moonfall (2022)*?

The local neighbourhood. One star, eight planets, and a dwarf planet some people are still arguing about. Quite a small area in the grand scheme of things, but there's still a lot going on here...

1. What does Dave Bowman find orbiting Jupiter in *2001: A Space Odyssey (1968)*?

   A: A space baby
   B: A bigger monolith
   C: A human skeleton
   D: God

2. In *Silent Running (1972)*, what are the space freighters intended to preserve?

   A: Earth's oceans
   B: Earth's animals
   C: The last humans
   D: Forests

3. Who starred in the cop-in-outer-space movie, *Outland (1981)*?

   A: Charlton Heston
   B: Sean Connery
   C: Sigourney Weaver
   D: Clint Eastwood

4. Which of Jupiter's moons is mankind forbidden from landing on in *2010: The Year We Make Contact (1984)*?

   A: Europa
   B: Titan
   C: Io
   D: Callisto

5. The titular ship in *Event Horizon (1997)* arrives at the planet Neptune after travelling to which star?

   A: Alpha Centauri
   B: Proxima Centauri
   C: Wolf 359
   D: Epsilon Eridani

6. The year 2000 saw two films about missions to Mars released. What were they?

   A: *The Martian*
   B: *Capricorn One*
   C: *Mission to Mars*
   D: *Red Planet Mars*
   E: *Stranded*
   F: *Red Planet*

7. In *Ghosts of Mars (2001)*, which actor and rapper played James 'Desolation' Williams?

A: Ice Cube

B: Ice-T

C: Snoop Dogg

D: Marky Mark

8. On their way to Earth's sun, what planet does the ship in *Sunshine (2007)* pass?

9. What does the lifeform found in *The Last Days on Mars (2013)* do to humans it comes into contact with?

A: Turns them into zombies

B: Blinds them

C: Makes them telepathic

D: Eats their flesh

10. In *Europa Report* (2013), what space phenomena knocks out *Europa One*'s communications?

A: A micrometeor

B: Cosmic rays

C: A black hole

D: A solar storm

11. What vegetable does Matt Damon's character grow on the moon in *The Martian (2015)*?

A: Carrots

B: Potatoes

C: Onions

D: Cabbage

12. Who is Brad Pitt's character searching for in *Ad Astra (2019)*?

A: His brother

B: His father

C: His uncle

D: His best friend

1. Aside from Dave Bowman, Frank Poole and the computer HAL, how many crew are aboard the Jupiter mission in *2001: A Space Odyssey (1968)*?
   A: Two
   B: Three
   C: Four
   D: Five

2. In *Silent Running (1972)*, the space freighters are branded with the logo of which real-world company?

3. Which of Jupiter's moons is *Outland (1981)* set on?
   A: Europa
   B: Callisto
   C: Io
   D: Ganymede

4. What process do the monoliths start within Jupiter in *2010: The Year We Make Contact (1984)*?

5. What prototype faster-than-light engine powers the *Event Horizon (1997)*?

6. What existing property was *Mission to Mars (2000)* based on?

7. In *Red Planet (2000)*, Gallagher builds a radio using parts from which Mars rover?

8. *Ghosts of Mars (2001)* is rumoured to have originally been a vehicle for which hero of John Carpenter's previous films?

9. In *Sunshine (2007)*, disaster strikes when the ship changes course and the navigator forgets to carry out which task?

10. What mission does *The Last Days on Mars (2013)* show the last days of?

11. What is the last image broadcast from the ship in *Europa Report (2013)* before communications are cut off completely?

12. What is the name of the marooned astronaut in *The Martian (2015)*?

13. What wild and extremely angry animal is set loose on a space station in *Ad Astra (2019)*?

    A: A gorilla

    B: A chimpanzee

    C: A baboon

    D: An orangutan

1. In the Danish silent movie, *A Trip to Mars (1918)* what is the Mars mission's ship called?

2. Which piece of music was used in *2001: A Space Odyssey (1968)* and was later played during the BBC's coverage of the moon landings?

3. What was the name of the decommissioned aircraft carrier that served as the set for the space freighter *Valley Forge's* interiors in *Silent Running (1972)*?

4. What is the name of the mining base's doctor in *Outland (1981)*?

5. The author of the books that *2001: A Space Odyssey* and *2010: The Year We Make Contact (1984)* are based on, Arthur C. Clarke, also wrote two other sequels. What years do they take their titles from?

6. In *Event Horizon (1997)*, after being thrown into space by an explosion, what does Cooper use to propel himself back to the ship?

7. What sort of society is the Martian colony in *Ghosts of Mars (2001)*?

8. After the crew in *Sunshine (2007)* completes their mission, which frozen city do we see the sun begin to shine over?

9. Who is the first member of the mission to die in *Europa Report (2013)*?

10. What is the name of the project Clifford McBride is working on in *Ad Astra (2019)*?

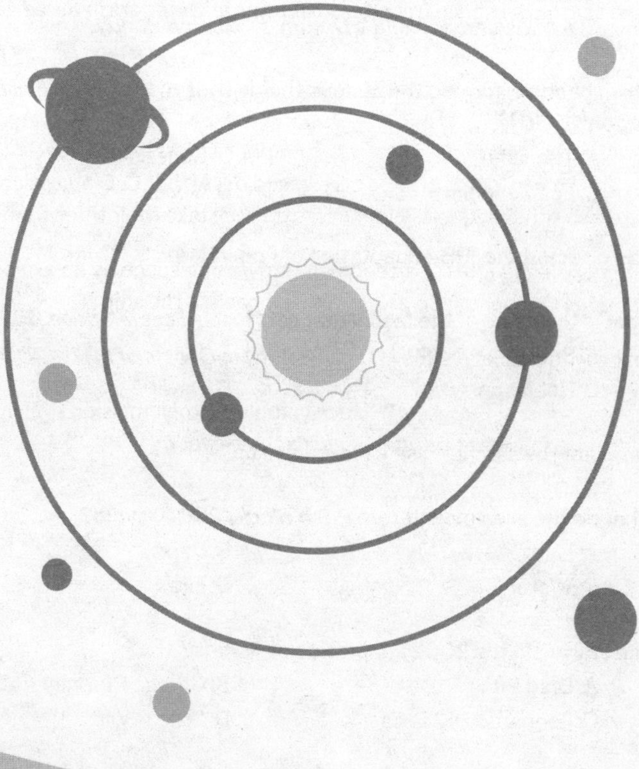

Now we're cooking with dilithium! These quizzes cover places you can only reach by sneaking past the speed of light when Einstein isn't looking, or maybe taking a very long and very cold nap...

1. *Forbidden Planet (1956)* is a science fiction reworking of which Shakespearean play?

A: *The Tempest* B: *Othello*
C: *A Midsummer Night's Dream* D: *Coriolanus*

2. Which band performed the famous theme song to the movie *Flash Gordon (1980)*?

A: The Who B: Genesis
C: Led Zeppelin D: Queen

3. Who directed the 1984 adaptation of Frank Herbert's *Dune*?

4. What is the name of the family that gets lost in *Lost in Space (1998)*?

A: Smith B: Jones
C: Robinson D: Davis

5. Complete the catchphrase - 'Never give up!'

6. What do the alien monsters in *Pitch Black (2000)* avoid?

A: Light B: Dark
C: Water D: Fire

7. Who starred in the 2002 adaptation of *Solaris*?

A: Brad Pitt B: George Clooney
C: Leonardo DiCaprio D: Bruce Willis

8. In *The Hitchhiker's Guide to the Galaxy (2005)*, who designed Earth's fjords?

A: Slartibartfast B: Zaphod Beeblebrox
C: Oolon Colluphid D: Gag Halfrunt

9. During the training exercise in *Ender's Game (2013)*, where is the gate?

A: Up | B: Down
C: Forward | D: Back

10. When the astronauts in *Interstellar (2014)* visit the ocean world, they are gone for only a few hours. How many years have passed on the ship while they were gone?

A: 2 years | B: 12 years
C: 23 years | D: 30 years

11. In *Dune (2021)*, which resource do the Atreides need to mine from the desert planet?

A: Oil | B: Unobtainium
C: Water | D: Spice

12. What is the last name of Paul Atreides' swordmaster, Duncan, played by Jason Momoa in *Dune (2021)*?

A: Ohio | B: Idaho
C: Texas | D: Connecticut

13. Who played the psychopathic Feyd-Rautha in *Dune: Part Two (2024)*?

A: Matt Smith | B: Austin Butler
C: Jared Leto | D: Alexander Skarsgård

14. In *Dune: Part Two (2024)*, Paul Atreides takes the new name 'Muad'Dib' as he lives among the Fremen people. What animal does this name refer to?

A: A sandworm | B: A trapdoor spider
C: A mouse | D: A lion

DEEP SPACE

1. The actor who played the spaceship captain in *Forbidden Planet (1956)* would go on to play which comedic police detective?

2. In the movie *Doctor Who and the Daleks (1965)*, what people are the Daleks' archenemies?

3. Which author wrote the novel that *Solaris (1972)* and *Solaris (2002)* were based on?

4. In *Dark Star (1974)*, what does Lieutenant Doolittle do with a piece of debris as he falls towards an unstable planet?

5. In *Flash Gordon (1980)*, what sport does Flash play?

   A: Polo

   B: American Football

   C: Basketball

   D: Baseball

6. In *Dune (1984)*, Gurney Halleck is played by which future *Star Trek* actor?

7. What surprising use do ice cubes have in *The Ice Pirates (1984)*?

   A: Narcotics

   B: Construction materials

   C: Currency

   D: Fuel

8. Who is the only actor to resume their role in *Lost in Space (1998)* from the original series?
   - A: Guy Williams
   - B: Bill Mumy
   - C: Dick Tufeld
   - D: Jonathan Harris

9. Complete the catchphrase – 'By Grabthar's Hammer...'

10. In *Pitch Black (2000)* what is the name of the surgery Riddick has to implant eyes capable of night vision?

11. *Dune (2021)* takes its title from the Fremen name of the desert planet. What does the Imperium call it?

12. What is the Gom Jabbar in *Dune (2021)*?
    - A: A box
    - B: A test
    - C: A poison needle
    - D: A political title

13. What house does Paul Atreides discover his mother descends from in *Dune: Part Two (2024)*?

14. Who plays Gurney Halleck in *Dune: Part Two (2024)*?

1. What is the name of the planet in *Forbidden Planet (1956)*?

2. *Terrore nello spazio (1965)* or 'Terror in Space' was released to American audiences under what name?

3. In *Flash Gordon (1980)*, the titular character is played by Sam J. Jones. But who played the character in the original 1930s film serials?

4. There have been two big screen adaptations of Frank Herbert's *Dune*, but which director, working with legends such as Chris Foss and H.R. Giger, famously failed to bring his *Dune* adaptation to the screen?

5. In *Lost in Space (1998)*, which organisation is behind the Jupiter Two mission?

6. What item does the cast of *Galaxy Quest (1999)* have to find a replacement for to make their starship work?

7. What weapon appears in *The Hitchhiker's Guide to the Galaxy (2005)* movie, but not any other version of the story?

8. What is the name of the medieval planet in *Hard to Be a God (2013)*?

9. In *Ender's Game (2013)*, what is the name of the insectoid alien species?

10. What is the name of the supermassive blackhole in *Interstellar (2014)*?

11. What is the shocking way the Fremen leader Stilgar pays tribute to Duke Leto Atreides in *Dune (2021)*?

12. In *Dune: Part Two (2024)* the Emperor of the Imperium is played by Chrisopher Walken. But which music video also starred Christopher Walken while referencing *Dune* in its lyrics?

TIME TRAVEL

Next to 'Space Travel' and 'Creating New Life That Immediately Tries to Kill You', 'Time Travel' is one of the foundational pillars of science fiction. It gives us the opportunity to venture back into history and see it with modern eyes, the ability to travel to the future and see where current trends might take us, and yet still the first thing most people want to do is go and murder their own grandfather...

BACKWARDS IN TIME

Whether you want to witness history firsthand or simply relive your youth, these are stories about swimming upstream in the river of time.

1. *A Connecticut Yankee in King Arthur's Court (1949)* is based on a novel by which 19th century author?

   A: H.G. Wells
   B: Jules Verne
   C: Mark Twain
   D: Charles Dickens

2. In *Somewhere in Time (1980)*, how does Christopher Reeve travel backwards in time?

   A: Hypnosis
   B: A doorway into the past
   C: He is put in a coma
   D: Stepping into a picture

3. In *Back to the Future (1985)*, what speed must the time machine reach before it can travel through time?

   A: 60 miles per hour
   B: 88 miles per hour
   C: 90 miles per hour
   D: 120 miles per hour

4. In *Bill & Ted's Excellent Adventure (1989)*, what is the name of Bill and Ted's world-saving band?

   A: Wyld Stallyns
   B: The Pinheads
   C: Bill and Ted
   D: The Beetles

5. What year does Marty McFly travel to in *Back to the Future Part III (1990)*?

   A: 1885
   B: 1895
   C: 1865
   D: 1900

6. Which Python directed *12 Monkeys (1995)*?

   A: Eric Idle
   B: Michael Palin
   C: Graham Chapman
   D: Terry Gilliam

7. In the Michael Crichton adaptation, *Timeline (2003)*, what war do the archaeology students travel to?

A: The Crusades

B: The Hundred Years' War

C: The War of the Roses

D: The Thirty Years' War

8. In *The Time Traveller's Wife (2009)*, what is the name of the time traveller?

A: Aaron Guest

B: Henry DeTamble

C: Frederick Robinson

D: Julian Anderson

9. What year do the characters travel back to in *Hot Tub Time Machine (2010)*?

A: 1984

B: 1985

C: 1986

D: 1987

10. In *Hot Tub Time Machine (2010)*, who plays the mysterious hot tub repairman?

A: Matthew Broderick

B: Thomas F. Wilson

C: Chevy Chase

D: Bill Murray

11. In *Safety Not Guaranteed (2012)*, what magazine receives the personals ad that the film takes its name from?

A: Seattle Magazine

B: Backwoods Home Magazine

C: Home & Garden Magazine

D: Time Magazine

BACKWARDS IN TIME

1. Which famous crooner plays the Connecticut Yankee in *A Connecticut Yankee in King Arthur's Court (1949)*?

2. *La Jetée (1962)* is the inspiration for which post-apocalyptic time travel movie?

    A: *Time Bandits (1981)*

    B: *The Terminator (1984)*

    C: *12 Monkeys (1995)*

    D: *Looper (2012)*

3. Where does Marty McFly meet Doc Brown to test his time machine in *Back to the Future (1985)*?

4. What is the mall called in *Back to the Future* when Marty returns at the end of the film?

5. Name three of the historical figures Bill and Ted recruit for their history report in their *Excellent Adventure*

6. What name does Marty McFly go by in *Back to the Future Part III (1990)*?

    A: John Wayne

    B: Clint Eastwood

    C: Gary Cooper

    D: Paul Newman

7. In *12 Monkeys (1995)*, who is the environmental activist Cole suspects of releasing the virus?

8. What 600-year-old item do the archaeology students in *Timeline (2003)* discover that convinces them time travel is possible?
   A: A bifocal lens
   B: Modern dentures
   C: A pocket watch
   D: A ballpoint pen

9. Up until 2024, including *The Time Traveller's Wife (2009),* how many films has Rachel McAdams appeared in where her character has travelled through time?

10. In *Safety Not Guaranteed (2012)*, why does Kenneth originally want to travel backwards in time?

BACKWARDS IN TIME

1. In the movie *Turn Back the Clock (1933)*, what happens to the protagonist before he finds himself reliving his younger days?

2. In *A Connecticut Yankee in King Arthur's Court (1949)*, Hank is able to escape execution by predicting what event?

3. In *La Jetée (1962)*, what event does the protagonist witness as a child?

4. In *Back to the Future (1985)*, what planet does Marty McFly pretend to be from to scare his father?

5. What school do Bill and Ted attend in *Bill & Ted's Excellent Adventure (1989)*?

6. Which band plays at the clock tower ceremony in *Back to the Future Part III (1990)*?

7. In *12 Monkeys (1995)*, what period does Cole travel to before arriving in 1996?

8. From Henry's perspective, in what year do he and Clare first meet in *The Time Traveller's Wife (2009)*?

9. In *Hot Tub Time Machine (2010)* Crispin Glover plays Phil the bellhop in both time periods. What body part does his character lose between those periods?

10. What vehicle is the time machine in *Safety Not Guaranteed (2012)* built into?

FORWARDS IN TIME

Whether you are travelling by time machine, flying at relativistic speeds, or simply falling into a hypersleep module by mistake, these questions are about people who have a glimpse of the future - or people from the past seeing just how badly we mucked things up today.

1. In *The Time Machine (1960)*, what two groups of humanoids does the time traveller discover in the distant future?

   A: Morlocks
   B: Troglodytes
   C: Ardanans
   D: Eloi
   E: Na'avi
   F: Mutoids

2. In the movie, *Beyond the Time Barrier (1960)*, what future year does the hero find themselves in?

   A: 1997 B: 2000
   C: 2019 D: 2024

3. In *The Time Travelers (1964)*, how do the three scientists travel to the future?

   A: Suspended animation
   B: A time portal
   C: Travelling close to the speed of light
   D: A malfunctioning teleportation device

4. In *Time After Time (1979)*, which two 19th-century historical figures find themselves in present-day San Francisco?

   A: H.G. Wells
   B: Queen Victoria
   C: Charles Dickens
   D: Jack the Ripper
   E: Sweeney Todd
   F: Isambard Kingdom Brunel

5. *The Philadelphia Experiment (1984)* concerns an urban myth about which real naval vessel?

A: The USS *Eldridge*

B: The USS *Philadelphia*

C: The *Mary Celeste*

D: The USS *Enterprise*

6. In *Flight of the Navigator (1986)*, how many years is David missing?

A: Six years

B: Eight years

C: Ten years

D: Twelve years

7. In *Back to the Future Part II (1989)*, what year does Doc take Marty McFly and Jennifer to?

A: 2012　　B: 2015

C: 2016　　D: 2020

8. In *Demolition Man (1993)*, Sylvester Stallone and Wesley Snipes' characters are placed into suspended animation in 1996. In what year are they woken up?

A: 2032　　B: 2096

C: 2127　　D: 2996

9. Who stars in the 2002 remake of *The Time Machine*?

A: Ethan Hawke

B: Brad Pitt

C: Guy Pearce

D: Shia LaBeouf

10. In *Idiocracy (2005)*, how long is Luke Wilson's character frozen in suspended animation?

A: 100 years　　B: 200 years

C: 500 years　　D: 1000 years

FORWARDS IN TIME

1. In *The Time Machine (1960)*, what weapon are people fearful of in the (then) future year of 1966?

2. What experimental aircraft does Major Bill Allison fly in *Beyond the Time Barrier (1960)*?

3. In the future, where do the survivors of the human race try to escape to in *Time Travelers (1964)*?
   A: Underground
   B: Mars
   C: Alpha Centauri
   D: Earth's past

4. What essential time machine component does Stevenson fail to take to the future in *Time After Time (1979)*?
   A: The time crystal
   B: The fluid link
   C: The non-return key
   D: The flux capacitor

5. In what year did *The Philadelphia Experiment (1984)* take place?
   A: 1939
   B: 1943
   C: 1945
   D: 1950

6. Who plays the NASA intern Carolyn McAdams in *Flight of the Navigator (1986)*?

7. What film is playing at the cinema of the future in *Back to the Future Part II (1989)*?

    A: *Terminator 9*

    B: *Star Wars Episode XI*

    C: *Jaws 19*

    D: *Casablanca 2*

8. What is the name of Sylvester Stallone's character in *Demolition Man (1993)*?

9. How is Simon Wells, the director of *The Time Machine (2002)*, related to the author of the original novel?

10. After awakening from suspended animation in *Idiocracy (2005)*, what hospital does Joe Bauers check into?

FORWARDS IN TIME

1. What is the name of the time traveller in *The Time Machine (1960)*?

2. What is the name of the futuristic city in *Beyond the Time Barrier (1960)*?

3. What year do *The Time Travellers (1964)* initially travel to?

4. In *Time After Time (1979)*, what restaurant does Malcolm McDowell's character first visit on arriving in 1979?

5. Having found themselves in 1984, what city do the protagonists of *The Philadelphia Experiment (1984)* choose to visit?

6. What TV show does David discover was cancelled during his absence in *Flight of the Navigator (1986)*?

7. What book of future knowledge does Marty acquire (and lose) in *Back to the Future Part II (1989)*?

8. What is the name of the mega city that Sylvester Stallone's *Demolition Man (1993)* character finds himself in when he is unfrozen in the future?

9. What is the name of the holographic librarian in *The Time Machine (2002)*?

10. According to his barcode ID, what is Luke Wilson's character's name in *Idiocracy (2005)*?

CHANGING HISTORY

It's time to get the flowcharts out for these movies. Branching timelines, fading photographs, paradoxes both grandfather and bootstrap, these are the movies where people start meddling with causality, and things are will have previously been going to get complicated quickly.

1. Who stars as the titular cop in *Timecop (1994)*?

    A: Peter Weller | B: Keanu Reeves
    C: Jean-Claude Van Damme | D: Steven Seagal

2. In *Frequency (2000)*, Jim Caviezel's character is able to talk to his dad in the past. What job does his father do?

    A: Firefighter | B: Police officer
    C: Paramedic | D: Truck driver

3. Where do the two tech entrepreneurs keep their accidentally-invented time machine in *Primer (2004)*?

    A: A university | B: Their garage
    C: A storage facility | D: Their basement

4. Who stars in the 2004 time travel movie *The Butterfly Effect*?

    A: Chris Pine | B: Zac Efron
    C: Robert Pattinson | D: Ashton Kutcher

5. In *Deja Vu (2006)*, Denzel Washington's character prevents a bombing on what form of public transport?

    A: A plane | B: A train
    C: A ferry | D: The underground metro

6. In *Frequently Asked Questions About Time Travel (2009)*, which room do the characters enter to travel through time?

    A: The gents' toilet | B: The ladies' toilet
    C: The disabled toilet | D: Another, non-toilet location

7. In *Looper (2012)*, Joe is played by which *two* actors?

A: Joseph Gordon-Levitt | B: Andrew Garfield
C: Robert Pattinson | D: Adrien Brody
E: Bruce Willis | F: Billy Bob Thornton

8. In *About Time (2013)*, what is the first thing Tim Lake wants to do with his time travel powers?

A: Get rich | B: Get a girlfriend
C: Prevent disasters | D: Become famous

9. In *Tenet (2020)*, what is the name of the process that allows people to experience time backwards?

A: Inversion | B: Reversion
C: Palindroming | D: Looping

Mini round – Time Loops!

1. What song is Phil woken up by every morning in *Groundhog Day (1993)*?

A: 'I Got You Babe' by Sonny & Cher
B: 'The One and Only' by Chesney Hawkes
C: 'Downtown' by Petula Clark
D: 'Back in Time' by Huey Lewis and the News

2. In *Source Code (2011)*, Colter Stevens keeps reliving a bombing on a train heading to which city?

A: San Francisco | B: Chicago
C: Detroit | D: Washington D.C.

3. In *Edge of Tomorrow (2014)*, Bill Cage starts his time loop waking up at which airport?

A: John F Kennedy | B: Frankfurt
C: Gatwick | D: Heathrow

4. In *Palm Springs (2020)*, Andy Samberg and Akiva Schaffer's characters are trapped in a time loop at what event?

A: A wedding | B: A birthday party
C: A high school reunion | D: A bar mitzvah

1. In *Timecop (1994)* Max Walker is sent to 1929 to stop his former partner from profiting from which historic event?

2. In *Frequency (2000)*, John Sullivan prevents his dad's death in a fire, only to find he died of what cause?

    A: Car accident
    B: Lung cancer
    C: Murder
    D: Heart attack

3. Before they accidentally build a time machine, what are the protagonists of *Primer (2004)* trying to build?

4. What is the name of the time-travel-enabling surveillance programme used in *Deja Vu (2006)*?

    A: Cinderella
    B: Snow White
    C: Sleeping Beauty
    D: Rapunzel

5. What is the group of unhinged fans called who try to alter history in *Frequently Asked Questions About Time Travel (2009)*?

6. Why does the crime syndicate in *Looper (2012)* send people back in time to kill them?

7. What event must a time traveller never travel back past in *About Time (2013)*?

8. What abandoned town is the 'Algorithm' taken to in *Tenet (2020)*?

Mini round – Time Loops!

1. What town does Phil end up stranded in in *Groundhog Day (1993)*?

2. In *Source Code (2011),* Colter Stevens takes on someone else's identity in the past. What job do they do?

   A: Architect

   B: Doctor

   C: Teacher

   D: Cop

3. Emily Blunt's character Rita, goes by which nickname after being caught in a time loop in *Edge of Tomorrow (2014)*?

4. In *Palm Springs (2020)*, what is the name of the third time looped character who constantly hunts Nyles?

1. What year is it in the future setting of *Timecop (1994)*?

2. What is the name of the nurse-murdering serial killer that John and Frank inadvertently save in *Frequency (2000)*?

3. What is one of the Aarons building at the end of *Primer (2004)*?

4. In *Deja Vu (2006)*, what location does Doug Carlin travel back to in order to survive the time travel process?

5. In *Frequently Asked Questions About Time Travel (2009)*, what does Ray become known as in the future?

6. In *Looper (2012)*, what is the crime lord Joe works for in the future known as?

7. How many times does Tim decide to live each day at the end of *About Time (2013)*?

8. What is the name of John David Washington's character in *Tenet (2020)*?

Mini round – Time Loops!

1. What date is Groundhog Day?
2. According to Dr Rutledge, what does the machine in *Source Code (2011)* use to reconstruct past events?
3. In *Edge of Tomorrow (2014)*, the alien Omega turns out to be beneath which art gallery?
4. What date is the wedding in *Palm Springs (2020)*?

OTHER REALITIES

Space and time are only the beginning. There are vistas of possibility out there, from universes and dimensions beyond our own, to worlds at the microscopic scale, or wrapped up within the depths of the human psyche. These quizzes will take you to places that aren't on any map, but which will make you see your own reality through new eyes...

What is 'Real' anyway? Is that air you're breathing? Is the chair beneath you made of real atoms? Or are you just a brain in a jar, dreaming these things while a computer makes you answer sci-fi movie trivia questions?

1. In *Total Recall (1990)*, Doug Quaid is a ____ who has false memories implanted to make him believe he is a ____.
   - A: Garbage man
   - B: Astronaut
   - C: Construction Worker
   - D: Scientist
   - E: Cop
   - F: Factory worker
   - G: Spy
   - H: Miner

2. In *The Lawnmower Man (1992)*, Jobe Smith is the first human subject to be experimented on with intelligence-boosting drugs and virtual reality after a similar regime was tried on which animal?
   - A: White mice
   - B: A chimpanzee
   - C: A dolphin
   - D: A pig

3. In *Virtuosity (1995)*, police have to chase down SID, a rogue VR character made from the worst serial killers in history. What does SID stand for?
   - A: Strong, Insidious, Deadly
   - B: Synthetic Infiltration Diagnostic
   - C: Sadistic, Intelligent, Dangerous
   - D: Silicon Insight Differentiator

4. Truman stars in *The Truman Show*, but who stars in the film *The Truman Show (1998)*?

5. Which of these pills will reveal the truth about *The Matrix (1999)*?

A: The red pill

B: The blue pill

6. In *The Thirteenth Floor (1999)*, Hannon Fuller has invented a virtual reality simulation of Los Angeles in which year?

A: 1937

B: 1955

C: 1963

D: 1999

7. In *Vanilla Sky (2001)*, what must David do to wake up from his simulation?

A: Click his heels together

B: Call 'tech support'

C: Shoot himself

D: Jump off a building

8. In *Inception (2010)*, Cobb can tell whether or not he is dreaming by –

A: Rolling a weighted dice

B: Spinning a spinning top

C: Pinching himself

D: Opening a random book

9. What is the virtual world of *Ready Player One (2018)* known as?

A: PLAYGROUND

B: DREAM

C: OASIS

D: 2REAL

VIRTUAL REALITIES

1. What Philip K. Dick novel is *Total Recall (1990)* based on?

2. When *The Lawnmower Man (1992)* explains his plan to evolve into a being of pure energy, what does he say will signal his 'birth'?

3. Who plays SID in *Virtuosity (1995)*?

4. In *The Truman Show (1998)*, what is Truman's surname?

   A: Rogers

   B: Anderson

   C: Burbank

   D: Bentham

5. In *The Matrix (1999)*, machines keep humans trapped in a simulation so they can use them as what?

6. In *eXistenZ (1999)*, what is the name of the terrorist group fighting against virtual reality companies?

   A: Realists

   B: Sensorists

   C: Actualists

   D: Platonists

7. In *The Thirteenth Floor (1999)*, what year is it *outside* the simulation?

8. *Vanilla Sky (2001)* is a remake of which Spanish film? You may give the title in English or Spanish.

9. In *Eternal Sunshine of the Spotless Mind (2004)*, can you remember the name of the memory editing company?

10. Including limbo, but not including the waking world, how many levels of dream do the characters go through during the job in *Inception (2010)*?

    A: Three

    B: Four

    C: Five

    D: Six

11. What does Wade Watts call his in-game avatar in *Ready Player One (2018)*?

12. What is the name of the idyllic company town that is not what it seems in *Don't Worry Darling (2022)*?

1. In *Total Recall (1990)*, what is Quaid told his name was before the memory implantation?

2. Which author sued to have his name removed from the credits for *The Lawnmower Man (1992)*?

3. Who directed *The Truman Show (1998)*?

4. Before *The Matrix (1999)*, which William Gibson-penned film featuring virtual reality did Keanu Reeves star in?

5. What is Neo's given name inside *The Matrix (1999)*?

6. In *eXistenZ (1999)*, the organic game system works by plugging into which part of your body?

7. What novel is *The Thirteenth Floor (1999)* loosely based on?

8. What is the song used to wake the characters up from every level of the dream at once in *Inception (2010)*?

9. Which of these films is <u>not</u> referenced in *Ready Player One (2018)*?
    - A: *Monty Python and the Holy Grail (1975)*
    - B: *Smokey and the Bandit (1977)*
    - C: *E.T. The Extra-Terrestrial (1982)*
    - D: *Star Trek II: The Wrath of Khan (1982)*
    - E: *Back to the Future (1985)*
    - F: *Big Trouble in Little China (1986)*
    - G: *Robocop (1987)*

10. *Don't Worry Darling (2022)* was the first film to be shot at which famous house in Palm Springs, California?

OTHER REALMS

A selection box of other realities, hidden away within our own...

The Subterranean

The ground might seem solid beneath your feet, but there are entire worlds down there...

1. In *The Phantom Empire (1935)*, the singing cowboy Gene Autry discovers an unknown civilisation...

    A: In an abandoned gold mine

    B: Under his ranch

    C: Through a waterfall

    D: In an extinct volcano

2. In *Journey to the Center of the Earth (1959)*, the underground adventurers discover which lost city?

    A: Atlantis B: El Dorado

    C: Thule D: Lothal

3. What meat do the mysterious doppelgängers in *Us (2019)* eat?

    A: Human flesh B: Rabbit

    C: Chicken D: Rat

The Microscopic

Even the most mundane parts of your world become astounding when you're smaller than a bug.

4. How quickly does *The Incredible Shrinking Man (1957)* shrink?

    A: An inch an hour B: An inch a day

    C: An inch a week D: An inch a month

5. In *Fantastic Voyage (1966)*, a team of scientists and medical professionals shrink down to remove a blood clot in a scientist's....

    A: Heart B: Lungs

    C: Brain D: Kidneys

6. In *Innerspace (1987)* the pilot Tuck Pendleton is meant to be shrunk down and injected into a rabbit. Instead, he is injected into:

A: An accountant
B: A grocery store clerk
C: A video store clerk
D: A car salesman

The Liminal
Sometimes another world will brush against a place in our own, leaving it... changed.

7. In *Stalker (1979)*, which of these four people does <u>not</u> enter the zone?

A: The Stalker
B: The Writer
C: The Priest
D: The Professor

8. The Infected Zone in *Monsters (2010)* is created when a NASA probe crash lands in which country?

A: Mexico
B: Brazil
C: Chile
D: Ecuador

9. What is the name of the mysterious anomalous zone in *Annihilation (2018)*?

A: The Blur
B: The Expanse
C: The Shimmer
D: No Man's Land

10. In *Vivarium (2019)*, a couple stumble into a mysterious, otherworldly place that at first glance looks like...

A: A fairground
B: A housing estate
C: A zoo
D: A high street

The Subterranean

1. What is the name of the secret underground civilisation in *The Phantom Empire (1935)*?
    - A: Subterra
    - B: Murania
    - C: Invertia
    - D: Hadeonia

2. In *Journey to the Center of the Earth (1959)* what is the name of the original explorer who found the route to the centre of the Earth?

3. What name are the doppelgängers in *Us (2019)* known by?
    - A: The Tethered
    - B: Gangers
    - C: Dupes
    - D: Mirrors

The Microscopic

4. In the basement of his house, what creature must *The Incredible Shrinking Man (1957)* fight?

5. What is the name of the submarine in *Fantastic Voyage (1966)*?

6. In *Innerspace (1987)*, how is Tuck transferred from Jack to Lydia's body?

The Liminal

7. What book is *Stalker (1979)* based on?

8. Who wrote and directed *Monsters (2010)*?

9. When the mutated bear in *Annihilation (2018)* roars, which character does it sound like?

10. The behaviour of the estate agent creatures in *Vivarium (2019)* is foreshadowed by the depiction of what animal in the movie's opening scene?

    A: A cuckoo

    B: A spider

    C: A caterpillar

    D: Multiplying bacteria

The Subterranean

1. In *The Phantom Empire (1935)*, what resource does the villain, Professor Beetson, intend to steal from the underground civilisation?

2. What country do the explorers in *Journey to the Center of the Earth (1959)* go to, to find a volcano to descend through?

3. In the 1986 prologue to *Us (2019)*, the name of which film by the same director is carved into the entrance of the hall of mirrors?

The Microscopic

4. What is the name of the increasingly dangerous cat in *The Incredible Shrinking Man (1957)*?

5. Which science fiction legend wrote the official novelisation of *Fantastic Voyage (1966)*?

6. What is the name of the henchman who is shrunk and injected into Jack to find Tuck in *Innerspace (1987)*?

The Liminal

7. Inspired by the film *Stalker (1979)*, the name 'Stalkers' has been adopted by guides to which hazardous territory?

8. How long is *Monsters (2010)* set after NASA discovered alien life?

9. Who wrote the book that *Annihilation (2018)* is based on?

10. What street number do Tom and Gemma live at in *Vivarium (2019)*?

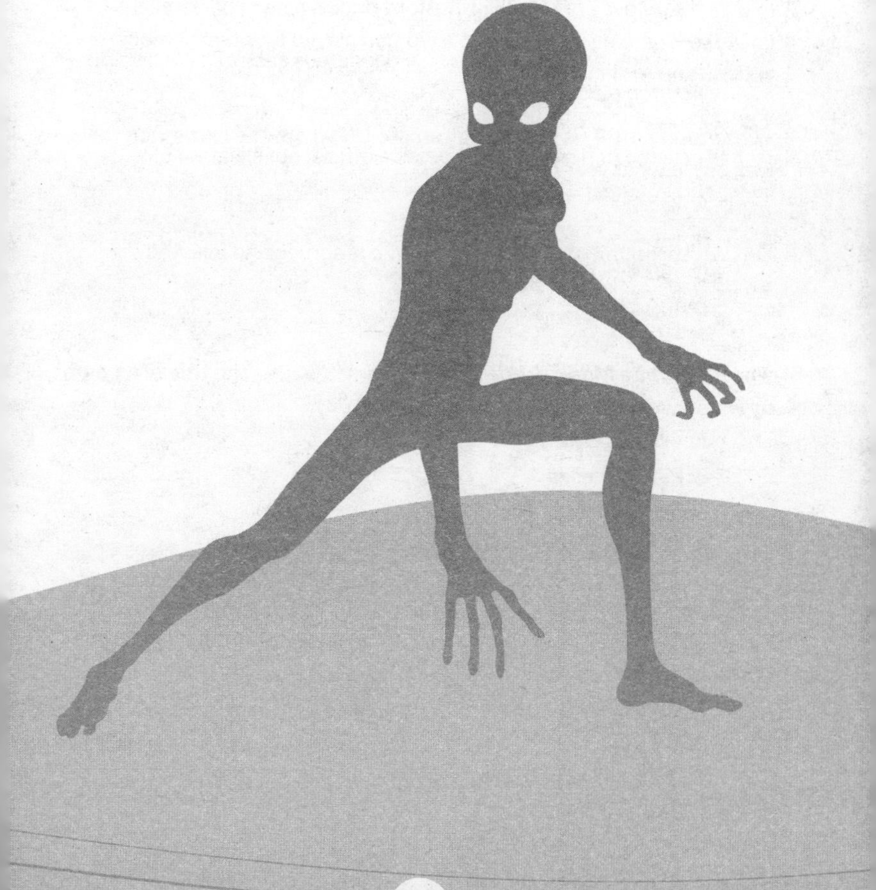

INFINITE DIMENSIONS!

Every choice you make sparks off a timeline where things turned out differently. The history you know is just one of infinite possibilities fanning out across the multiverse. So, if you get these questions wrong at least you know that somewhere, you were correct...

1. In *It Happened Here (1964)*, what year did Germany invade Britain?

    A: 1939

    B: 1940

    C: 1945

    D: 1950

2. In *Quest for Love (1971)*, Colin Trafford finds himself in a parallel universe where he is married to a woman played by which famous actress and romance novelist?

3. *Fatherland (1994)* is set in an alternate UK where the Nazis won the war, but in what year?

    A: 1954

    B: 1964

    C: 1984

    D: 1994

4. The film *White Man's Burden (1995)* ironically uses the title of a poem by which writer?

    A: Wilfred Owen

    B: Percy Shelley

    C: Rudyard Kipling

    D: William Wordsworth

5. In *Sliding Doors (1998)*, Helen Quilley's life branches down two different timelines depending on whether she gets through which pair of sliding doors?

    A: On a train

    B: On a lift

    C: On a bus

    D: At an airport

6. In the multiverse of *The One (2001)*, how many universes have a version of Jet Li's character?

    A: 42

    B: 125

    C: 461

    D: 1000

7. In *Coherence (2013)*, eight friends come into contact with their alternate duplicates after what astronomical event?

    A: Aurora Borealis

    B: A solar flare

    C: A distant supernova

    D: A comet

8. Which of these actors plays a Spider-Man who dies in *Into the Spider-Verse (2018)*?

    A: Jake Johnson

    B: Nicholas Cage

    C: Chris Pine

    D: Andrew Garfield

9. Can you remember which band nobody can remember in *Yesterday (2019)*?

10. What business does Evelyn run in *Everything Everywhere All at Once (2022)*?

    A: A takeaway

    B: A hair salon

    C: A key cutters and shoe repair shop

    D: A launderette

1. The influential alternate history movie *It Happened Here (1964)* takes its name as a reference to which 1936 antifascist novel?

2. *Quest for Love (1971)* is based on a short story by which noted British science fiction writer?

3. In *Fatherland (1994)*, who is the Queen of England?

4. Who plays the factory worker Louis Pinnock in *White Man's Burden (1995)*?

5. In one timeline of *Sliding Doors (1998)*, when James first meets Helen he shows himself to be funny and charming by quoting which Monty Python line?

6. In the opening scenes of *The One (2001)*, who is seen on TV as President of the Unites States?
   A: George W. Bush
   B: Al Gore
   C: Hillary Clinton
   D: Bob Dole

7. In *Coherence (2013)*, what colour glowsticks do the main versions of the characters carry?

8. In the end credits of *Into the Spider-Verse (2018)*, what item does Spider-Man Noir take back to show his own universe?

9. Which singer-songwriter does Jack best in a songwriting duel in *Yesterday (2019)*?

    A: Chris Martin

    B: Harry Styles

    C: Ed Sheeran

    D: Adele

10. What devastating baked good could destroy the multiverse in *Everything Everywhere All at Once (2022)*?

1. While *It Happened Here (1964)* was mostly cast with amateurs, which well-known actor, author and playwright played Doctor Richard Fletcher?

2. In the parallel universe of *Quest for Love (1971)*, who was the first person to climb Mount Everest?

3. In the alternate history of *Fatherland (1994)*, which two European territories are *not* Nazi-occupied?

4. What does Louis Pinnock's factory make in *White Man's Burden (1995)*?

5. At the end of *Sliding Doors (1998)*, how does Helen get hospitalised in both timelines?

6. What does MVA stand for in *The One (2001)*?

7. In *Coherence (2013)*, what teen drama does Nicholas Brendon's character say he starred in?

8. In *Into the Spider-Verse (2018)* and *Across the Spider-Verse (2023)*, what number is written on the back of the spider that bites Miles?

9. What British town is Jack from in *Yesterday (2019)*?

10. What does Evelyn do to download the skills of the singer version of herself in *Everything Everywhere All at Once (2022)*?

DYSTOPIAS

Science fiction is often thought of as prophetic, but usually it is not trying to predict the future but to shine a light on the problems in the present. So, it is alarming how close some of these stories get to the mark...

A collection of dark futures, where governments and businesses have turned society into a gigantic prison that looks like a twisted funhouse mirror reflection of our own time...

1. In *A Clockwork Orange (1971),* what is the name of sci-fi slang Alex and his friends speak?
   A: 1337 Spe4k
   B: Newspeak
   C: Nadsat
   D: Satnav

2. Dystopian sci-fi thriller *THX 1138 (1971)* is an early film by which franchise-launching space opera director?

3. What is the name of the monstrous driver played by David Carradine in *Death Race 2000 (1975)*?
   A: Grim Reaper
   B: Red Baron
   C: Frankenstein
   D: Road Rage

4. In *1984 (1984),* Winston Smith lives on Airstrip One. But which superpower is Airstrip One part of?
   A: Oceania
   B: Eurasia
   C: Eastasia
   D: Australasia

5. The dystopian satire *Brazil (1985)* takes place during which holiday season?
   A: Valentine's Day
   B: Easter
   C: Halloween
   D: Christmas

6. In *The Running Man (1987),* which of the following is <u>not</u> a nickname from one of the 'Stalkers' sent to hunt down Schwarzenegger's Ben Richards?

   A: Fireball

   B: Captain Freedom

   C: Dynamo

   D: Buzz Saw

   E: Nitro

   F: Subzero

7. What city does *Judge Dredd (1995)* police?

8. The veritable 'V' in *V for Vendetta (2005)* places a veneer across his visage of which vengeful villain?

9. In *Children of Men (2006),* what is the name of the immigrant-rights group that hires Theo to transport the only pregnant woman in the world?

   A: The Fugees

   B: The Human Project

   C: The Fishes

   D: The Ark of Art

10. The 2012 movie *Dredd* takes place almost entirely within one tower block. What is it called?

    A: Peach Trees

    B: Sunny Acres

    C: Paradise Towers

    D: Nakatomi Plaza

1. What do Alex and his droogs drink in *A Clockwork Orange (1971)*?

2. What is the name of the woman that THX 1138 falls in love with in *THX 1138 (1971)*?

   A: EVE 0320
   B: HUD 1993
   C: LUH 3417
   D: VHS 2006

3. What event preceded the Fascist American government seen in *Death Race 2000 (1975)*?

   A: World War III
   B: The World Crash of '79
   C: Occupation by the USSR
   D: Global famine

4. Which ministry does Winston Smith work for in *1984 (1984)*?

   A: The Ministry of Peace
   B: The Ministry of Truth
   C: The Ministry of Love
   D: The Ministry of Plenty

5. Who is arrested in the opening scene of *Brazil (1985)*?

6. Who was *supposed* to have been arrested in the opening scene of *Brazil*?

7. *The Running Man (1987)* is based on a novel written by Stephen King, but it was published under which pseudonym?

8. What is the United States of America called in *The Handmaid's Tale (1990)*?

9. Complete the advertising slogan from *Judge Dredd (1995)*: 'Eat recycled food. It's good for the environment'...

10. Who plays 'V' in *V for Vendetta* (2005)?
    A: James Purefoy
    B: Hugo Weaving
    C: Tom Hardy
    D: John Hurt

11. What is the name of the only pregnant woman in the world in *Children of Men (2006)*?

12. What is the name of the drug Ma-Ma is dealing in *Dredd (2012)*?

BIG BROTHER IS WATCHING YOU

1. Lemmy Caution is the hero of the dystopian sci-fi movie *Alphaville (1965)*, but the character was originally created by which crime author?

2. What is the name of the fictional technique used to reform Alex in *A Clockwork Orange (1971)*?

3. According to background radio chatter in *THX 1138 (1971)*, what does one driver think they ran over on the expressway?

4. Once you enter Pennsylvania, how many points do you get for running over a teenager in *Death Race 2000 (1975)*?

5. *1984 (1984)* is the final screen appearance of which well-respected actor?

6. What is the Portuguese title of the song *Brazil (1985)* takes its name from?

7. What year is *The Running Man* set in?

8. Which famous playwright is credited as the screenwriter of *The Handmaid's Tale (1990)* despite attempting to have his name removed from the credits?

9. In *Judge Dredd (1995)*, what is Judge Dredd's first name?

10. What is the secret police force in *V for Vendetta (2005)* known as?

11. *Children of Men (2006)* is loosely based on a book by which crime novelist?

12. In *Dredd (2012)*, how many stars does the American flag have?

EVERYTHING IS FINE! (HONEST)

The future needn't be all that grim! In fact, it can be positively bright! Take a look at these utopian visions where everything worked out okay. These are futures where we have managed to do away with modern ills, such as illness, crime, old people and feelings...

1. The movie *Fahrenheit 451 (1966)* takes its name from the temperature that:

    A: Water boils

    B: Paper burns

    C: Meat is safe to eat

    D: Steel melts

2. *Soylent Green (1973)* is made of people. But which other varieties of Soylent appear in the film? Choose all the correct answers.

    A: Soylent Red

    B: Soylent Yellow

    C: Soylent Blue

    D: Soylent Brown

3. In *Logan's Run (1976)*, people live a luxurious and hedonistic lifestyle, but only until they reach what age?

    A: 21

    B: 25

    C: 30

    D: 35

4. In the idyllic future of *Demolition Man (1993)*, what is the only restaurant brand left by 2032?

5. In *Gattaca (1997)*, Vincent Freeman disguises his genetic profile to get a job as a navigator on a mission to which moon?

    A: Europa

    B: Callisto

    C: Titan

    D: Phobos

6. In a future where feelings have been made illegal, the Clerics of *Equilibrium (2002)* police emotions through which fictional martial art?

    A: Gun Fu

    B: Gunjitsu

    C: Gun Kata

    D: Sho Gun

7. How many Precogs are there in *Minority Report (2002)*?

8. In *The Island (2005)*, why are the residents told they cannot leave the island?

    A: Climate change

    B: Pathogens

    C: A nuclear winter

    D: Asteroid collision

9. In *In Time (2011)*, how long is left on your clock when you reach your 25th birthday?

    A: 24 hours

    B: One month

    C: One year

    D: Five years

10. Match the *Divergent (2014)* faction to the quality it is supposed to represent.

Abnegation	Peaceful
Amity	Brave
Candor	Selfless
Dauntless	Intelligent
Erudite	Honest

EVERYTHING IS FINE! (HONEST)

1. At the end of *Fahrenheit 451 (1966)*, what book does Guy Montag choose to memorise?
   - A: *David Copperfield* by Charles Dickens
   - B: *Tales of Mystery and Imagination* by Edgar Allen Poe
   - C: *Around the World in 80 Days* by Jules Verne
   - D: *1984* by George Orwell

2. We all know that *Soylent Green* is made from people. But in the 1973 film, what is it advertised as made from?
   - A: Soy beans
   - B: Plankton
   - C: Lab-grown meat
   - D: Fungus

3. What is the name of the rite that people in *Logan's Run (1976)* must undergo when their life-clock runs out?

4. In *Demolition Man (1993)*, what three objects do people use instead of toilet paper?

5. In *Gattaca (1997)*, genetic analysis gives Vincent Freeman a projected lifespan of how long?
   - A: 24.3 years
   - B: 30.2 years
   - C: 35.9 years
   - D: 42.4 years

6. What is the name of the fictional country depicted in *Equilibrium (2002)*?
   - A: Libria
   - B: Freedonia
   - C: Tetragrammaton
   - D: Omelas

7. What is the name of Tom Cruise's Precrime cop in *Minority Report (2002)*?

A: Jonathan Anderson

B: James Amesdon

C: John Anderton

D: Jim Anguson

8. Which of Lincoln Six Echo's organs does his 'sponsor' need in *The Island* (2005)?

A: His kidneys

B: His heart

C: His liver

D: His lungs

9. In the future of *In Time (2011)*, everyone stops aging on their 25th birthday. But which of these cast members was actually 25 when the movie was released on 1 November 2011?

A: Justin Timberlake

B: Olivia Wilde

C: Amanda Seyfried

D: Vincent Paul Kartheiser

10. What city is *Divergent (2014)* set in?

A: Chicago

B: New York

C: San Francisco

D: Los Angeles

EVERYTHING IS FINE! (HONEST)

1. In H.G. Wells' own screenplay, *Things to Come (1936)*, what is the name of the group of engineers who establish world peace by flying over everyone and disseminating knock-out gas?
2. Who plays Guy Montag in *Fahrenheit 451 (1966)*?
3. What is the population of Earth in *Soylent Green (1973)*?
4. In *Logan's Run (1976)* what is Logan's numerical surname?
5. Who is the leader of the 'Scraps' resistance group in *Demolition Man (1993)*?
6. What does Jerome Eugene Morrow win an Olympic medal for in *Gattaca (1997)*?
7. What is the emotion-suppressing drug used in *Equilibrium (2002)*?
8. What is the murder weapon in the crime prevented at the start of *Minority Report (2002)*?
9. In *The Island (2005)*, what is Lincoln Six Echo's 'Sponsor' called?
10. What are *Divergent (2014)*'s two sequels called?

THE END OF THE WORLD! (AND WHAT COMES NEXT…)

A lot of humans are disturbed by the idea of the world carrying on without them long after their deaths. So please take some comfort in the possibility that it might not! Between a vast, cold and indifferent universe of hazards, and humanity's own predilection for self-destruction, honestly, it's pretty slim odds that we'll make it to the end of the week.

CLIMATE CATASTROPHE!

Since the invention of roofs, mankind has thought that technology will save us from our old enemy, the weather. It turns out the opposite is true.

1. In the global disaster movie *Deluge (1933)*, which of the following phenomena are <u>not</u> seen?

   A: Flooding

   B: Tornados

   C: Solar eclipse

   D: Earthquakes

2. In *The Day the Earth Caught Fire (1961)*, what causes the global climate disaster?

   A: Pollution

   B: Nuclear testing

   C: The Earth's magnetic poles reversing

   D: A solar flare

3. In *Quintet (1979)*, civilisation has collapsed following:

   A: A global drought

   B: A new ice age

   C: Global flooding

   D: Acid rain

4. Who starred in the legendary megaflop *Waterworld (1995)*?

5. Which city is overrun by tornadoes in *The Day After Tomorrow (2004)*?

   A: Washington D.C.

   B: New York

   C: Los Angeles

   D: San Francisco

6. What year is it at the beginning of *2012 (2009)*?

7. In *Beasts of the Southern Wild (2012)*, which prehistoric creature is released from the ice by rising temperatures?
   - A: Aurochs
   - B: Diprotodon
   - C: Mammoths
   - D: Megatherium

8. In *Snowpiercer (2013)* a new ice age forces the last remnants of humanity to take shelter aboard a giant, constantly travelling:
   - A: Zeppelin
   - B: Ship
   - C: Train
   - D: Aeroplane

9. Who plays Jake Lawson in *Geostorm (2017)*?

10. The futuristic noir movie, *Reminiscence (2021)* is set in which post-climate-change flooded city?
   - A: Detroit
   - B: San Francisco
   - C: Miami
   - D: Chicago

1. In *Deluge (1933)*, where do Martin, Helen and their children try to shelter from the storm?
   - A: The basement
   - B: A nearby quarry
   - C: An underground train station
   - D: A bomb shelter

2. In *The Day the Earth Caught Fire (1961)*, which paper does journalist Paul Stenning write for?
   - A: *The Daily Mail*
   - B: *The Daily Telegraph*
   - C: *The Daily Express*
   - D: *The Evening Standard*

3. Including the character of Ambrosia, how many players does a game of 'Quintet' have in the 1979 climate disaster movie of the same name?

4. In *Waterworld (1995)* what material does the Mariner use as currency?

5. Who directed *The Day After Tomorrow (2004)*?

6. In *2012 (2009)*, who plays struggling science fiction writer Jackson Curtis?

7. In *Beasts of the Southern Wild (2012), w*hat is the name of the community Hushpuppy lives in?

8. Which actress plays the tyrannical Minister Mason in *Snowpiercer (2013)*?

9. In Geostorm, which famously tall skyscraper is hit by a Tsunami?

   A: The Empire State Building

   B: The Burj Khalifa

   C: Shanghai Tower

   D: The Shard

10. Who plays the memory retrieval specialist Nick Bannister in the post-climate-change noir movie *Reminiscence (2021)*?

CLIMATE CATASTROPHE!

1. Which city do we see completely destroyed by the apocalyptic disasters of *Deluge* (*1933)*?

2. What are the two possible headlines seen at the end of *The Day the Earth Caught Fire (1961)*?

3. Which famous actor of stage and screen plays 'Essex' in *Quintet (1979)*?

4. In the extended edition of *Waterworld (1995)* where is the mythical 'Dry Land' revealed to be?

5. In *The Day After Tomorrow (2004)*, what famous New York public building do the characters take shelter in?

6. In *2012 (2009)*, what type of 'mutated' particle causes global flooding, earthquakes, volcanic eruptions and mega-tsunamis?

    A: Tachyons
    B: Neutrinos
    C: Positrons
    D: Photons

7. What is the name of the Oscar-nominated young actress who played Hushpuppy in *Beasts of the Southern Wild (2012)*?

8. At the end of *Snowpiercer (2013)*, what clue do the characters see that life can exist in the outside world?

9. What is the name of the system of weather control satellites responsible for the *Geostorm (2017)*?

10. Who wrote and directed the post-climate-change noir movie, *Reminiscence (2021)*?

PANDEMIC FEVER!

What's great about human civilisation is that no matter how many times it has ground to a halt because of a widespread disease outbreak, it will still call a movie about it 'Science Fiction'.

1. In *It's Great to Be Alive (1933)*, what segment of the population is wiped out by a deadly pandemic?

2. On which continent does the grass-killing virus in *No Blade of Grass (1970)* originate?

    A: Africa

    B: Asia

    C: North America

    D: South America

3. *The Crazies (1973)* was written and directed by which director more commonly known for zombie movies?

4. *Right at Your Door (2006)* portrays a dirty bomb attack on Los Angeles from the perspective of an out-of-work:

    A: Musician

    B: Writer

    C: Painter

    D: Chef

5. Which country in the British Isles is quarantined in *Doomsday (2008)*?

    A: England

    B: Scotland

    C: Wales

    D: Northern Ireland

6. Which actor played 'the Doctor's Wife', the only person immune to the epidemic of blindness in *Blindness (2008)*?

    A: Jodie Foster

    B: Julianne Moore

    C: Laura Dern

    D: Julia Roberts

7. Chris Pine appeared in the pandemic movie *Carriers (2009)* the same year as he starred in which major sci-fi franchise?

8. *The Exam (2009)* is about the final exam of a job interview for a company selling the only treatment for a viral pandemic. Which of these is not a rule of the exam?

   A: The candidates must not spoil their paper

   B: The candidates must not leave the room

   C: The candidates must not confer

   D: The candidates must not talk to the invigilator or the armed guard at the door

9. The pandemic thriller *Contagion (2011)* had a massive ensemble cast, but which of these actors did not appear in it?

   A: Matt Damon

   B: Laurence Fishburne

   C: Elliott Gould

   D: Mark Wahlberg

   E: Jude Law

   F: Marion Cotillard

10. *Isle of Dogs (2018)* sees all the dogs moved to a trash island after an outbreak of canine influence in which country?

PANDEMIC FEVER!

1. *No Blade of Grass (1970)* is an adaptation of which book?

2. What is the name of the deadly virus released in *The Crazies (1973)*?

   A: Janet
   B: Amy
   C: Judy
   D: Trixie

3. *The Year of the Plague* or *El año de la peste (1978)* is a loose, updated adaptation of a novel by which historical author?

   A: Mary Shelley
   B: Daniel Defoe
   C: Jules Verne
   D: Jonathan Swift

4. In *Right at Your Door (2006)*, Brad's quarantine is broken by what object being thrown through a door pane?

5. What is the name of the deadly virus in *Doomsday (2008)*?

6. What sort of doctor does Mark Ruffalo play in *Blindness (2008)*?

7. What are the three 'Rules' Brian comes up with to survive the pandemic in *Carriers (2009)*?

8. Who plays the invigilator for *The Exam (2009)* to decide who will work at the pharmaceutical company in that film?

9. The virus in *Contagion (2011)* draws genetic material from viruses that have infected which two other animals?

    A: Bats
    B: Birds
    C: Cows
    D: Pigs

10. Who directed the canine epidemic movie *Isle of Dogs (2018)*?

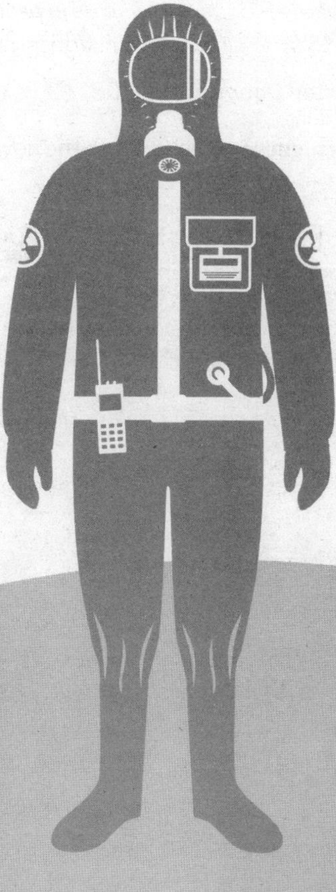

PANDEMIC FEVER!

1. What is the name of the deadly disease in *It's Great to be Alive(1933)*?
2. Who recorded the title song for the film *No Blade of Grass (1970)*?
3. What is the name of the city where the virus is unleashed in *The Crazies (1973)*?
4. Which noted magical realist author wrote the screenplay for *The Year of the Plague (1978)*?
5. What system does the virus in *Right at Your Door (2006)* attack?
6. Who directed *Doomsday (2008)*?
7. Which Portuguese novelist wrote the novel that *Blindness (2008)* is based on?
8. Where do the characters in *Carriers (2009)* try to reach to take shelter from the 'World Ender Virus'?
9. What is the name of the company that sells the palliative treatment for the virus in *The Exam (2009)*?

10. In *Contagion (2011)* a conspiracy theorist tries to promote a homeopathic cure derived from which yellow flowering plant?

11. Which stray dog in *Isle of Dogs (2018)* is voiced by Bryan Cranston?

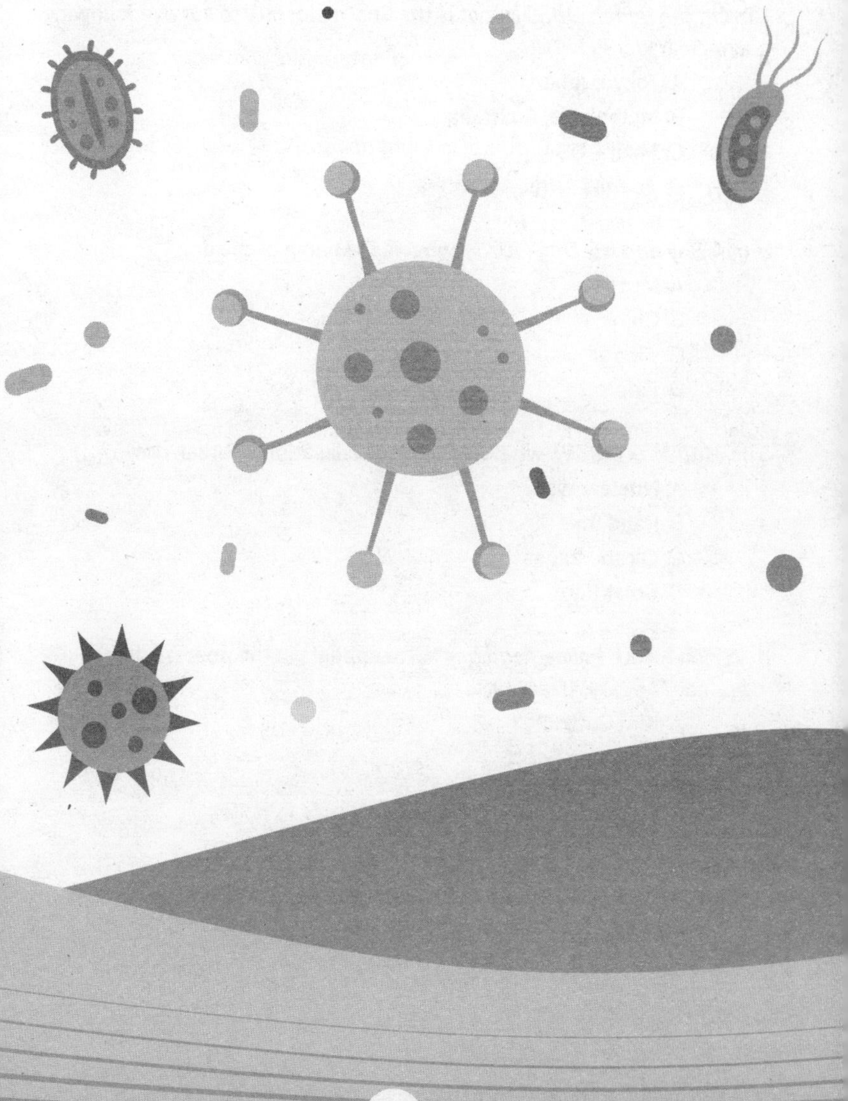

AFTER THE END

The worst has happened. The nukes have dropped. The resources we need to live are all gone. The deadly virus has run rampant through the streets. The great thing about people is that they are so optimistic their next question is, 'What happens next?'

1. In *On the Beach (1959)* what is the final major city to survive following a nuclear war?

   A: Tokyo, Japan

   B: Melbourne, Australia

   C: Miami, USA

   D: Buenos Aires, Argentina

2. In *A Boy and His Dog (1975)*, what is the name of the dog?

   A: Mutt

   B: Cujo

   C: Blood

   D: Fido

3. In *Mad Max (1979)*, what has caused civilisation to break down?

   A: Nuclear war

   B: Pandemic

   C: Oil shortages

   D: Solar flare

4. Which future *Police Academy* actor appears in the post-nuclear drama, *The Day After (1983)*?

   A: Kim Cattrall

   B: Donovan Scott

   C: Steve Guttenberg

   D: G.W. Bailey

5. The BBC TV movie, *Threads (1984)*, shows the effects of nuclear war on which northern British city?

   A: Manchester

   B: York

   C: Sheffield

   D: Durham

6. Who starred and directed in *The Postman (1997)*?

7. *The Road (2009)* is an apocalyptic tale based on the novel by which author best known for his Westerns?

8. What is the eponymous book in *The Book of Eli (2010)*?

   A: A Bible

   B: An Encyclopaedia

   C: *Das Kapital*

   D: *The Complete Works of Shakespeare*

9. In *The World's End (2013)*, starring Simon Pegg and Nick Frost, what is the one processed food that Andy misses after the apocalypse?

10. In *Mad Max: Fury Road (2015)*, what resource does the warlord Immortan Joe horde at his citadel?

    A: Petrol

    B: Water

    C: Food

    D: Electricity

AFTER THE END

1. Which famous dancing American actor played the Australian scientist, Julian Osborn in *On the Beach (1959)*?

2. What year is it when the characters in *A Boy and His Dog (1975)* are wandering the post-nuclear wasteland?

   A: 1996
   B: 2001
   C: 2016
   D: 2024

3. What is *Mad Max*'s surname?

4. Post-nuclear TV movie *The Day After (1983)* was directed by which filmmaker best known for his Star Trek movies?

5. The Italian post-apocalyptic action movie, *The New Barbarians (1983)*, or *I Nuovi Barbari*, was also known by what English title?

   A: *The New Warriors*
   B: *Warriors of the Wasteland*
   C: *Road Warriors*
   D: *The Warriors*

6. In *Threads (1984)*, where are you advised to put dead bodies while you are kept in your house's 'fallout room'?
    - A: Keep it in the room with you, sealed up
    - B: Move it to another room in the house
    - C: Take it outside and bury it
    - D: Take it outside and burn it

7. Before taking on the role of the titular delivery worker in *The Postman (1997)*, how does the unnamed traveller earn a living?
    - A: As a tinker and repairman
    - B: As a bounty hunter
    - C: By performing Shakespearean plays
    - D: As a fortune teller

8. Which *Lord of the Rings* actor plays the role of 'The Man' in *The Road (2009)*?

9. What electronic device does Eli carry with him in *The Book of Eli (2010)*?

10. When Immortan Joe's War Boys ride out in *Mad Max: Fury Road (2015)*, why do they take Max with them?

AFTER THE END

1. What is the name of the last US Naval submarine in *On the Beach (1959)*?
2. Which famously grouchy science fiction writer wrote the novella that *A Boy and His Dog (1975)* is based on?
3. What is the name of the car Max drives through *Mad Max (1979), Mad Max 2: The Road Warrior (1981)* and *Mad Max: Fury Road (2015)*?
4. Which city in Kansas is the setting of much of the action in *The Day After (1983)*?
5. What is the name of the ruthless gang who are the villains of *The New Barbarians (1983)*?
6. How many years past the nuclear exchange does *Threads (1984)* show us?
7. In *The Postman (1997)*, what is the name of the antagonist leader played by Will Patton?
8. Who plays the role of 'The Woman' in *The Road (2009)*?

9. Where does Eli take his book in *The Book of Eli (2010)*?

10. In *Mad Max: Fury Road (2015)*, name two of Immortan Joe's wives.

This is all getting a bit dour, but here's a funny thing. If you kill almost everyone, collapse civilisation, make food scarce and medicine impossible to come by, it's really depressing. Throw in a few billion walking corpses that want to eat you? Suddenly it's fun again!

1. In *The Last Man on Earth (1964)*, a lone human survivor is forced to fend off nightly attacks by undead monsters. But rather than zombies, in this movie the attackers are...

   A: Ghosts

   B: Vampires

   C: Werewolves

   D: Frankensteins

2. In *Night of the Living Dead (1968)*, what causes the dead to reanimate and attack the living?

   A: An alien virus

   B: Mutated bacteria

   C: Radiation from a crashed space probe

   D: Ancient magic

3. In *The Omega Man (1971)*, what is the name of the cult of plague victims that lay siege to the lone human survivor's home?

   A: Sons of the Atom

   B: Alphas

   C: The Family

   D: The Brotherhood

4. According to the tagline of *Dawn of the Dead (1978)*, when will the dead walk the Earth?

5. In the zombie movie (it is a zombie movie) *28 Days Later (2002)*, what lab animal is the Rage virus communicated to humans from?

   A: Rats

   B: Monkeys

   C: Bats

   D: Chimpanzees

6. What is the name of the pub Shaun and co. hole up at in *Shaun of the Dead (2004)*?
   - A: The World's End
   - B: The Winchester
   - C: The Nag's Head
   - D: The Crown

7. In *Fido (2006)*, what is the name of the company that makes zombie control collars?
   - A: Zom-B-Good
   - B: ZomCon
   - C: Laz-R-Us
   - D: Dead4U

8. In *Zombieland (2009)*, which Ghostbuster actor's house do the survivors take shelter in?

9. In *World War Z (2013)*, which organisation does Brad Pitt's character Gerry Lane work for?
   - A: Centre for Disease Control
   - B: World Health Organisation
   - C: United Nations
   - D: Central Intelligence Agency

10. How is the zombie infection communicated in *The Girl with All the Gifts (2016)*?
    - A: Virus
    - B: Bacteria
    - C: Fungus
    - D: Radiation

1. What is the name of the novel that *The Last Man on Earth (1964)*, and *The Omega Man (1971)* adapted, and which *Night of the Living Dead (1968)* took inspiration from?

2. What are the names of the siblings visiting the cemetery in the opening scene of *Night of the Living Dead*?

3. In *The Omega Man*, the mutants are caused by biological weapons in a war between which two states?

4. Which legendary make-up artist provided the zombie make-up for *Dawn of the Dead (1978)*?

5. In *28 Days Later (2002)*, which *Doctor Who* actor plays Major Henry West?

6. What sitcom did *Shaun of the Dead (2004)* actors Simon Pegg, Nick Frost and Jessica Hynes, as well as their director Edgar Wright, originally work together on?

7. Who plays the titular zombie in *Fido (2006)*?

8. In *Zombieland (2009)*, the zombie infection is a mutated form of what disease?

    A: Rabies

    B: Mad Cow Disease

    C: Bird Flu

    D: Ebola

9. Who wrote the book that *World War Z (2013)* is based on?

10. What are the zombie-like infected in *The Girl with All the Gifts (2016)* known as?

11. At the start of the film, where does the *Train to Busan (2016)* leave from?

    A: Seoul

    B: Incheon

    C: Ulsan

    D: Daejeon

1. Who plays Robert Morgan in *The Last Man on Earth (1964)*?

2. How many times is the word 'Zombie' used in *Night of the Living Dead (1968)*?

3. When the cult captures Robert Neville in *The Omega Man (1971)*, which stadium do they attempt to execute him in?

4. Which shopping mall was *Dawn of the Dead (1978)* filmed in?

5. In *28 Days Later (2002)*, which London hospital does Jim wake up in?

6. Which two songs come on the jukebox in *Shaun of the Dead (2004)* when it is 'on random'?

7. In *Fido (2006)*, what is the name of the heavily fortified community Timmy lives in?

8. Where is Woody Harrelson's character from in *Zombieland (2009)*?

9. In *World War Z (2013)*, which country does Gerry go to first to track the origin of the zombie infection?

10. What is the name of *The Girl with All the Gifts (2016)*?

11. What is the name of the animated prequel to *Train to Busan (2016)*?

SPACE COLLISION

While a lot of these films say that we are likely to be killed by manmade climate change, nuclear weapons, genetically engineered viruses or just basic human cruelty, let's look on the bright side. It is entirely possible that, at any moment, space might reach out and kill you for no reason.

1. One of the earliest films to depict such a scenario, *La Fin du monde* or *End of the World (1931)*, sees Earth on a collision course with which comet?

   A: Halley's Comet

   B: Hale-Bopp

   C: Lexell's Comet

   D: Caesar's Comet

2. *When Worlds Collide (1951)* opens with a quote from which book of the Bible?

   A: Genesis

   B: Job

   C: Exodus

   D: Revelation

3. What causes the giant asteroid cluster to head for Earth in *The Day the Sky Exploded (1958)*?

   A: Solar winds

   B: Earth's gravity

   C: An accidental rocket explosion

   D: Cosmic rays

4. In *Meteor (1979)*, the efforts to prevent a fatal collision with planet Earth are led by which former James Bond actor?

5. In *Armageddon (1998)*, the US government responds to an imminent asteroid collision by recruiting a team of what kind of specialists?

   A: Coal miners

   B: Vulcanologists

   C: Oil rig workers

   D: Construction workers

6. In *Deep Impact (1998)*, who plays the President of the United States of America?

7. How wide is the asteroid approaching Earth in *Seeking a Friend for the End of the World (2012)*?

   A: 5 miles

   B: 10 miles

   C: 70 miles

   D: 100 miles

8. In *The Wandering Earth (2019),* Earth is fitted with massive engines to pilot it away from an expanding sun, but on the way it inadvertently ends up on a collision course with which planet?

   A: Mars

   B: Jupiter

   C: Saturn

   D: Neptune

9. Where does the comet-collision movie, *Greenland (2020),* get its name from?

   A: The survival shelter is in Greenland

   B: The asteroid is the size of Greenland

   C: The government can save as many people as the population of Greenland

   D: Because after the comet wipes out humanity Earth will be a 'Green Land'

10. In *Don't Look Up (2021)*, how much notice does Earth have that a comet is going to hit us?

    A: Five years

    B: One year

    C: Six months

    D: Twelve weeks

SPACE COLLISION

1. What is the name of the rogue star set to crash into Earth in *When Worlds Collide (1951)*?

   A: Bellerophon

   B: Beta

   C: Bacchus

   D: Bellus

2. What is the name of the planet Earth sends an ark to in *When Worlds Collide*?

   A: Zorya

   B: Zyra

   C: Zorro

   D: Zeta

3. What title was *The Day the Sky Exploded (1958)* or *La Morte Viene Dallo Spazio*, released under in the UK?

   A: *Skies of Fire*

   B: *The Explosion Heard Round the World*

   C: *Death Comes from Outer Space*

   D: *Doom from Above*

4. The asteroid heading towards Earth in *Meteor (1979)* is named after which musician from Greek mythology?

5. Which band performed the signature track 'I Don't Wanna Miss a Thing' for the soundtrack of *Armageddon (1998)*?
   A: Aerosmith
   B: Bon Jovi
   C: Bryan Adams
   D: AC/DC

6. What does E.L.E. stand for in *Deep Impact (1998)*?

7. Which actors play the two 'friends' in *Seeking a Friend for the End of the World (2012)*?

8. *The Wandering Earth (2019)* is based on a story by which Chinese science fiction writer?

9. In *Greenland (2020)*, where does the first comet fragment land?

10. In *Don't Look Up (2021)*, how much are the assets in the comet projected to be worth?
    A: $500 billion
    B: $32 trillion
    C: $140 trillion
    D: $280 trillion

SPACE COLLISION

1. *La fin du monde* or *The End of the World (1931)* was based on which French novel?

2. What is the name of the magnate who funds the ark rockets in *When Worlds Collide (1951)*?

3. In *The Day the Sky Exploded (1958)*, what is the name of Earth's first astronaut?

4. What are the USA and USSR's nuclear weapons satellites called in *Meteor (1979)*?

5. During a stop to refuel on the way to blowing up the asteroid in *Armageddon (1998)*, the crew of the *Freedom* inadvertently blow-up which space station?

6. What is the name of the spaceship sent to save mankind from an asteroid collision in *Deep Impact (1998)*?

7. What is the name of the asteroid in *Seeking a Friend for the End of the World (2012)*?

8. What is the name of the computer controlling the space station in *The Wandering Earth (2019)*?

9. The comet in *Greenland (2020)* is called 'Clarke', a reference to which Arthur C. Clarke novel about an imminent asteroid collision?

10. What does President Orlean die of in *Don't Look Up (2021)*?

NOBODY SAW THIS COMING!

While many filmmakers have tried to foresee the end of the world, it is always worth bearing in mind that whatever actually kills us all will be a total surprise.

1. What legendary name directed the ornithocalypse movie, *The Birds (1963)*?

   A: Orson Welles

   B: Stanley Kubrick

   C: Ingmar Bergman

   D: Alfred Hitchcock

2. What colour mankini does Sean Connery wear for the majority of the post-apocalyptic movie *Zardoz (1974)*?

   A: Green

   B: Yellow

   C: Orange

   D: Pink

3. In *The Quiet Earth (1985)*, almost all of humanity is wiped out by a 'wireless global energy grid' experiment under what name?

   A: Project Flashlight

   B: Operation Flashlight

   C: The Twilight Device

   D: The Liberty Torch

4. Which country is the post-apocalyptic cannibalism movie, *Delicatessen (1991)* set in?

5. *Reign of Fire (2002)* shows us a post-apocalyptic Britain overrun by which mythical animal?

6. In *The Core (2003)* a team of scientists must travel to the centre of the Earth when its molten core...

   A: Cools down

   B: Gets too hot

   C: Stops spinning

   D: Reverses polarity

7. After being stranded in a grocery store by *The Mist (2007)*, a group of survivors band together to go to which other nearby facility?

A: A telephone box

B: A gun store

C: A pharmacy

D: A police station

8. Who directed *The Happening (2008)*?

A: M. Night Shyamalan

B: Sam Raimi

C: Jordan Peele

D: James Wong

9. Which language carries the infection in *Pontypool (2008)*?

A: English

B: French

C: Spanish

D: German

10. What name is given to the mobile-phone-infected zombies in *Cell (2016)*?

A: Phonies

B: Phoners

C: Phonists

D: Phonics

11. Which monsters are mutated by the monsterpocalypse of *Love and Monsters (2020)*?

A: Invertebrates

B: Cold-blooded creatures

C: Herbivores

D: Amphibians

1. Who starred as Mitch Brenner in *The Birds (1963)*?

2. The mysterious, all-commanding floating stone head that *Zardoz (1974)* takes its name from is in turn named after which children's book?

3. Which country was *The Quiet Earth (1985)* set in?

4. What is Louison's occupation before he accepts the fatal job advertisement in *Delicatessen (1991)*?

   A: Magician
   B: Acrobat
   C: Lion Tamer
   D: Clown

5. In *Reign of Fire (2002)*, human survivors have taken shelter in which castle?

   A: Bamburgh Castle
   B: Barnard Castle
   D: Dover Castle
   D: Warwick Castle

6. What is the name of the hypothetical material necessary to the world-saving mission in *The Core (2003)*?

7. Which state is the Stephen King adaptation *The Mist (2007)* set in?

8. What is said to have caused the mass suicides in *The Happening (2008)*?
    A: Cell phone masts
    B: Plant toxins
    C: Subsonic vibrations
    D: Earth's magnetic field

9. What is the name of the book *Pontypool (2008)* is based on?

10. In *Cell (2016)*, what is the name of the figure people are seeing in their dreams?
    A: 'Thin Man'
    B: 'Smiling Man'
    C: 'Raggedy Man'
    D: 'Shadow Man'

11. What is the name of the bunker's cow in *Love and Monsters (2020)*?
    A: Daisy
    B: Buttercup
    C: Gertie
    D: Matilda

NOBODY SAW THIS COMING!

1. *The Birds (1963)* was an adaptation of a short story by which author?
2. In *Zardoz (1974)*, what is the name of the luxurious abode of the 'Eternals'?
3. What do the three survivors in *The Quiet Earth (1985)* have in common?
4. Jean-Pierre Jeunet, the director of *Delicatessen (1991)*, would go on to direct which entry in the *Alien* franchise?
5. In *Reign of Fire (2002)*, Quinn Abercromby re-enacts (and claims to have made up) the plot of which movie?
6. What do all the people who die in the opening scenes of *The Core (2003)* have in common?
7. *The Mist (2007)* was director Frank Darabont's third Stephen King adaptation. What were his first two?
8. In what city does *The Happening (2008)* start to occur at the end of the film?
9. What sort of speech must you avoid to protect yourself from the infection in *Pontypool (2008)*?

10. What is the name of the mythical safe haven in *Cell (2016)*?

11. What is the name of the asteroid whose destruction causes the monsterpocalypse of *Love and Monsters (2020)*?

OH THE TRANSHUMANITY

While there are many science fiction stories about fantastic places or marvellous inventions, there have also been many stories about how humanity itself might change. What would a person do with the ability to fly, or read minds, or turn invisible? Commit crimes? Or maybe save the world?

QUICKFIRE ROUND: MATCH THE INVISIBLE MAN!

Match up each of these invisible actors with the movie they appeared in. To help, we've added pictures!

1. *The Invisible Man (1933)*
2. *The Invisible Man Returns (1940)*
3. *The Invisible Woman (1940)*
4. *Invisible Agent (1942)*
5. *Abbot & Costello Meet the Invisible Man (1951)*
6. *The Amazing Transparent Man (1960)*
7. *Memoirs of an Invisible Man (1992)*
8. *Hollow Man (2000)*
9. *The Invisible Man (2020)*

A. *Claude Rains*

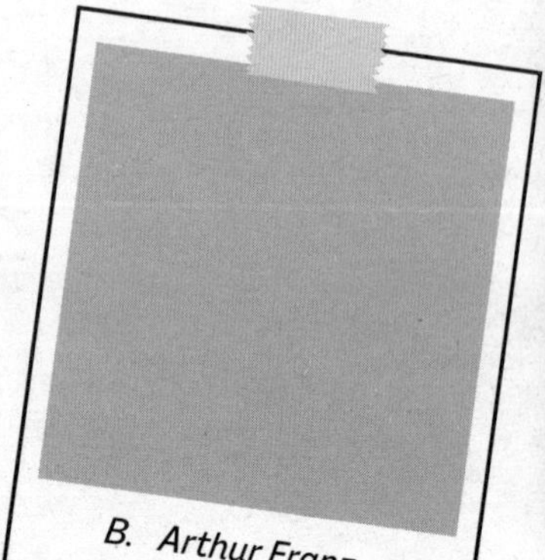

B. *Arthur Franz*

C. *Chevy Chase*

D. *Douglas Kennedy*

E. Jon Hall

F. Kevin Bacon

G. Oliver Jackson-Cohen

H. Vincent Price

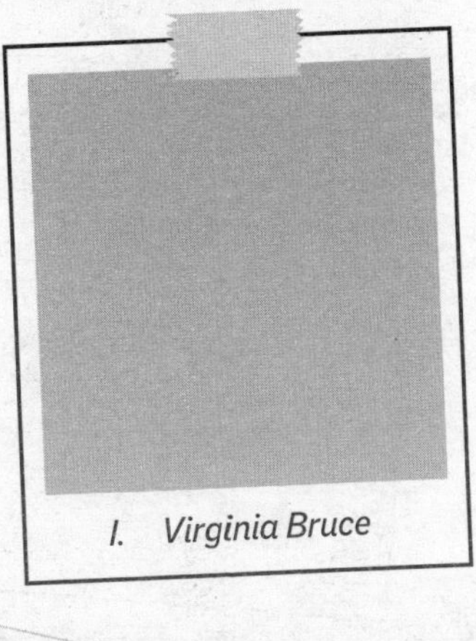

I. Virginia Bruce

It is said that humans only use 10% of the brain's potential capacity. It isn't true, but people have made a *lot* of movies about it.

1. Before the eponymous character in *Charly (1968)* undergoes a surgical procedure to make himself more intelligent, the procedure is tested on Algernon, who is what kind of animal?
   - A: Chimpanzee
   - B: Mouse
   - C: Rat
   - D: Dog

2. Both *Scanners (1981)* and *The Dead Zone (1983)* concern people discovering they have mind powers, and were directed by which body-horror-loving filmmaker?

3. Which famous Christopher plays the role of Johnny Smith in *The Dead Zone (1983)*?
   - A: Christopher Plummer
   - B: Christopher Walken
   - C: Christopher Lee
   - D: Christopher Lloyd

4. In *Dreamscape (1984)*, the psychic Alex Gardner must save which high-ranking figure by entering their dreams?
   - A: The Pope
   - B: The British Prime Minister
   - C: The President of the United States
   - D: The head of the CIA

5. In *Powder (1995)* Jeremy 'Powder' Reed has what distinguishing physical feature?
   - A: He has an extra finger
   - B: He is albino
   - C: Two sets of eyelids
   - D: Pointed ears

6. In *Phenomenon (1996)*, what job does George Malley do before he gains his mysterious powers?

   A: Auto mechanic

   B: Plumber

   C: Janitor

   D: Mailman

7. In *Next (2007)*, how far can Cris Johnson usually see into the future?

   A: 24 hours

   B: 60 minutes

   C: 5 minutes

   D: 2 minutes

8. In *Limitless (2011)*, Eddie Morra finds the experimental mind-expanding drug kicks in while he is talking to his:

   A: Girlfriend

   B: Boss

   C: Landlady

   D: Loan shark

9. When the drug CPH4 allows *Lucy (2014)* to mentally travel through time, what is the earliest chronological event she witnesses?

   A: Her own birth

   B: The human ancestor Australopithecus known as 'Lucy'

   C: The dinosaurs

   D: The Big Bang

10. In *Split (2016)*, how many personalities does Kevin Wendell Crumb have?

    A: 5

    B: 12

    C: 23

    D: 45

1. Before he undergoes the procedure, where does the main character of *Charly (1968)* work?

2. How many of the telepathic *Scanners (1981)* are known to exist?
   A: 95
   B: 129
   C: 237
   D: 341

3. In *The Dead Zone (1983)* Johnny Smith can see glimpses of people's past and futures when he...
   A: Sees them
   B: Hears them
   C: Touches them
   D: Smells them

4. In *Dreamscape (1984)*, who played the villainous Bob Blair?

5. Which actor plays Donald Ripley in *Powder (1995)*?

6. In *Phenomenon (1996)*, which language does George learn in minutes with his improved intelligence?
   A: Spanish
   B: Portuguese
   C: Mandarin
   D: French

7. Who plays Cris Johnson in *Next (2007)*?

8. By the end of *Limitless (2011)*, what political role is Eddie campaigning for?

9. What country is *Lucy (2014)* studying in at the start of the film?

10. Which M. Night Shyamalan film is *Split (2016)* a stealth sequel to?

1. Who played Charly Gordon in *Charly (1968)* and the earlier TV adaptation of the same story, 'The Two Worlds of Charlie Gordon' in *The United States Steel Hour*?

2. What is the name of the experimental drug responsible for creating the *Scanners (1981)*?

3. What is the name of the senate candidate whose apocalyptic future Johnny Smith glimpses in *The Dead Zone (1983)*?

4. In *Dreamscape (1984),* what educational institute do the people who recruit Alex claim to be from?

5. In *Powder (1995)*, what happens to Jeremy 'Powder' Reed's pregnant mother to give him supernatural powers?

6. What is found to have caused George Malley's powers in *Phenomenon (1996)*?

7. What time does Cris Johnson foresee Liz Cooper walking into the diner in *Next (2007)*?

8. What is the name of the brain-expanding drug that Eddie takes in *Limitless (2011)*?

9. In *Lucy (2014)*, which people naturally produce small amounts of the fictional drug CPH4?

10. In *Split (2016)*, which of the following are not Kevin's alters?

    A: Barry

    B: Pauline

    C: Hedwig

    D: Mr Glass

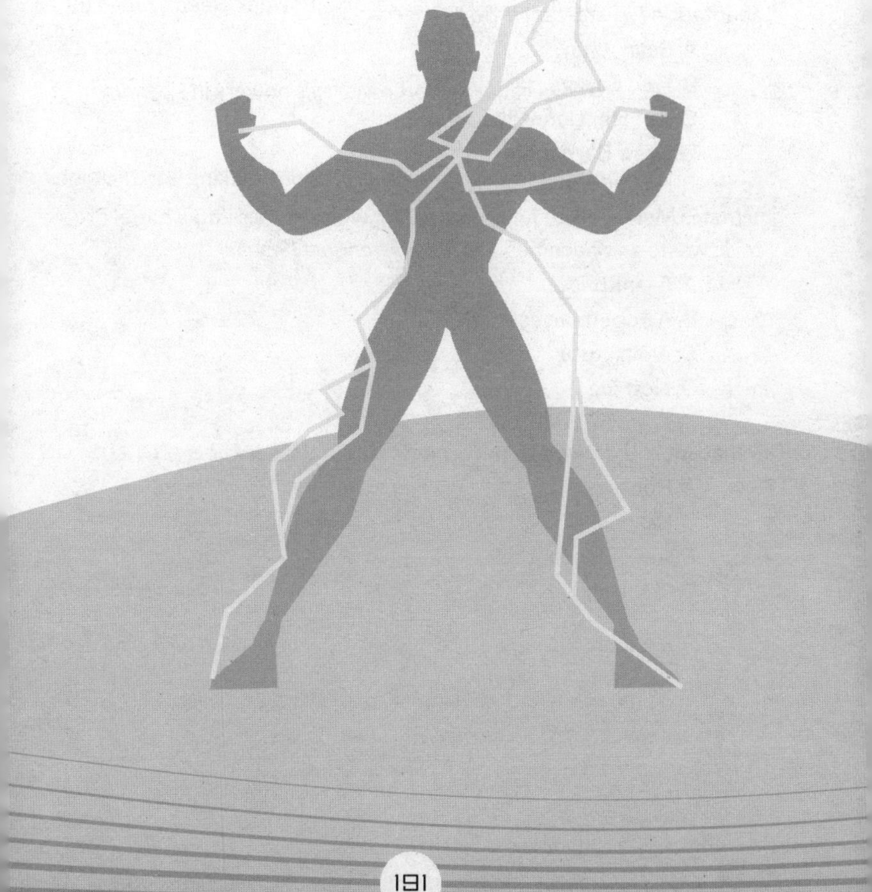

INCREDIBLE SUPERPOWERS

Teleportation, invisibility, the ability to control fire – with these great powers must also come... other things.

1. What is the name of *The Invisible Man (1933)*?
    - A: Dan Sparent
    - B: Stu Storm
    - C: Jack Griffin
    - D: Sebastien Caine

2. In *Superman (1978)*, what planet is Superman from?

3. Which child star played the titular character in the Stephen King adaptation *Firestarter (1984)*?
    - A: Sean Astin
    - B: Fred Savage
    - C: Jennifer Connelly
    - D: Drew Barrymore

4. What is Melvin 'Ferd' Junko III wearing when he falls into a barrel of toxic waste and becomes *The Toxic Avenger (1984)*?
    - A: A janitor's uniform
    - B: A Superman costume
    - C: A pink tutu
    - D: Nothing

5. What sport did David Dunn formerly play in *Unbreakable (2000)*?
    - A: Hockey
    - B: Baseball
    - C: American football
    - D: Track and field

6. In *Jumper (2008),* what is the name of the secret organisation that hunts down people with teleportation powers?

A: Templars
B: Paladins
C: Inquisitors
D: Conquistadors

7. What superpowered individual does Chris Evans play in the movie *Push (2009)*?

A: Pinky Stein
B: Hook Waters
C: Nick Gant
D: Victor Budarin

8. In *Watchmen (2009)* Doctor Manhattan burns the symbol for which element into his own forehead?

A: Carbon
B: Hydrogen
C: Oxygen
D: Uranium

9. Who plays Neil Clarke, the randomly picked individual given ultimate power, in *Absolutely Anything (2015)*?

A: Martin Freeman
B: Simon Pegg
C: Chris Pratt
D: Rob Schneider

10. What state is *Brightburn (2019)* set in?

A: Kansas
B: Missouri
C: Nebraska
D: Colorado

1. Who directed *The Invisible Man (1933)*?

2. In *Superman (1978)*, what town does Clarke grow up in?

3. What is the technical name for the fire-controlling powers Charlie exhibits in *Firestarter (1984)*?

4. What town, named after the studio that made the film, is *The Toxic Avenger (1984)* set in?

   A: Tromaberg

   B: Tromaton

   C: Tromapolis

   D: Tromaville

5. What kind of vehicle crash first alerts David Dunn to his powers in *Unbreakable (2000)*?

6. Which *Star Wars* prequel actor plays David Rice in *Jumper (2008)*?

7. What is the name of the shadowy organisation that hunts powered individuals in *Push (2009)*?
    - A: The Department
    - B: The Division
    - C: The Bureau
    - D: The Agency

8. In *Watchmen (2009)* what is the name of the 40s crime-fighting force that precedes the Watchmen?

9. The surviving members of which classic sketch show troupe reunited to voice the power-bestowing aliens in *Absolutely Anything (2015)*?

10. What is the only substance that can harm Brandon, the superpowered child in *Brightburn (2019)*?
    - A: Water
    - B: Rocks from his home planet
    - C: Pieces of his spaceship
    - D: Gold

1. *The Invisible Man (1933)* is the origin of which stock sci-fi villain phrase?
   A: 'But I am invincible!'
   B: '"Mad!" they called me! Mad!'
   C: 'I meddled in things that man must leave alone.'
   D: 'Nobody can defeat me!'

2. Christopher Reeve plays Superman in the 1978 film, but who was the first actor to take on the role on screen?

3. What nickname is the Department of Scientific Intelligence known by in *Firestarter (1984)*?

4. What was the real name of 'Mr Glass' in *Unbreakable (2000)*?

5. Which world-famous landmark does David leave Roland stranded near in *Jumper (2008)*?

6. In *Push (2009)*, what power do 'Watchers' have?

7. What was the name of Doctor Manhattan before he gained his powers?

8. What is the first thing Neil Clarke wishes for in *Absolutely Anything (2015)*?

9. At the end of *Brightburn (2019)*, a news reporter places Brandon alongside a selection of other superpowered menaces, including the protagonist of which film by *Brightburn's* producer, James Gunn?

10. Who plays The Toxic Avenger in the 2023 remake of the film?

MAD SCIENCE!

Aliens and monsters and robots and other dimensions are all great, but at the end of the day, science fiction is all about the science. Maybe not science in the strictly documented, peer-reviewed sense. Definitely not science in the sense of something that would ever get past an ethics board. Perhaps not even science that would pass a high school exam, but the important thing is – somebody is wearing a white coat.

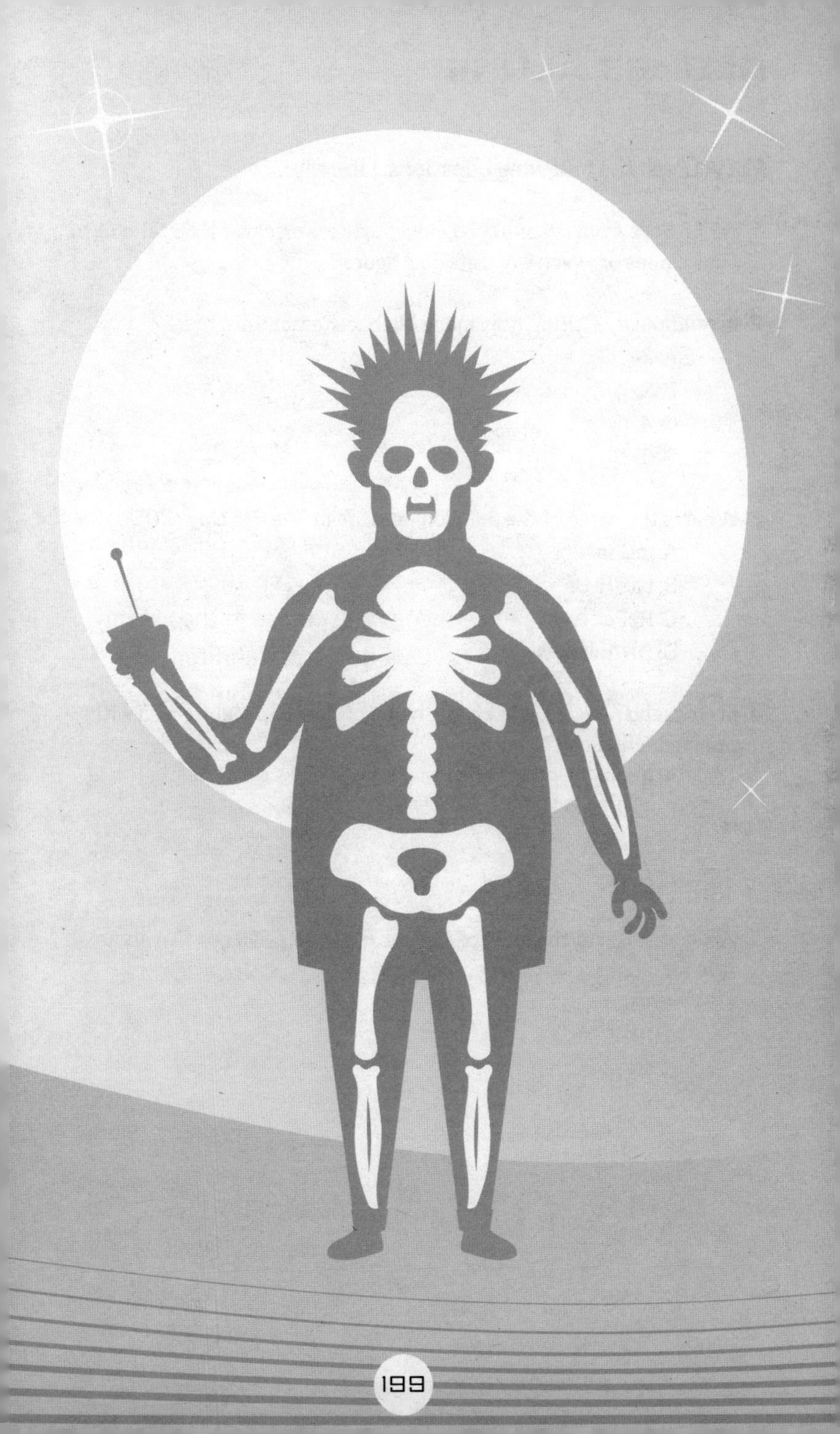

CLONES ALONE

Ask yourself the following questions. Literally.

1. In *The Boys from Brazil (1978)*, investigators discover a secret plot to raise clones of which evil historical figure?

2. In *Multiplicity (1996)*, how many Michael Keatons are there?
   A: 2
   B: 3
   C: 4
   D: 5

3. What is the name of the pet cloning store in *The 6th Day (2000)*?
   A: InGen
   B: Laz-R-Us
   C: RePet
   D: DNAnimals

4. In *Godsend (2004)*, what is the name of the child resurrected with cloning technology?
   A: Adam
   B: Jack
   C: Mark
   D: Ben

5. What year is it at the start of *Never Let Me Go (2010)*, a film about a farm for clones used as organ donors?
   A: 1978
   B: 1985
   C: 1994
   D: 2010

6. In *Oblivion (2013)*, what city does Jack have memories of from his previous life?

   A: New York

   B: Venice

   C: Paris

   D: Edinburgh

7. Which actor is digitally de-aged to play his own clone in *Gemini Man (2019)*?

8. In *Swan Song (2021)*, what name is given to Cameron Turner's clone?

   A: Adam

   B: Jack

   C: Mark

   D: Ben

9. In *Dual (2022)*, which former *Doctor Who* companion must fight their own clone to the death?

   A: Billie Piper

   B: Freema Agyeman

   C: Karen Gillan

   D: Jenna Coleman

10. In *They Cloned Tyrone (2023)*, who plays Tyrone?

    A: Jamie Foxx

    B: John Boyega

    C: Kiefer Sutherland

    D: J. Alphonse Nicholson

CLONES ALONE

1. In *The Boys from Brazil (1978)*, why are the clones' adoptive fathers murdered after the clones' 13th birthdays?
   - A: To cover up that their children are clones
   - B: Because the original figure's father died when he was 13
   - C: Because their adoptive fathers were abusive
   - D: So that the clones do not realise they are adopted

2. Which of these is not a clone in *Multiplicity (1996)*?
   - A: Lance
   - B: Rico
   - C: Doug
   - D: Lenny

3. Who plays charter pilot Adam Gibson, and charter pilot Adam Gibson's clone in *The 6th Day (2000)*?

4. Who plays the geneticist who offers to clone Jessie and Paul's dead child in *Godsend (2004)*?

5. Match up the clones. Which young actor played which older actor in the 2010 clone movies *Never Let Me Go* and *Womb*?

Andrew Garfield	Tristan Christopher
Keira Knightley	Isobel Meikle-Small
Carey Mulligan	Ella Purnell
Matt Smith	Charlie Rowe

6. Which moon is Jack told the human race has evacuated to in *Oblivion (2013)*?
   A: Titan
   B: Europa
   C: Ganymede
   D: Earth's Moon

7. How many clones does Henry Brogan have in *Gemini Man (2019)*?

8. Why does Cameron Turner have himself cloned in *Swan Song (2021)*?
   A: As an organ donor
   B: To replace him when he dies
   C: To do the jobs he doesn't want to do
   D: To provide an alibi

9. How does Sarah's clone kill her in *Dual (2022)*?
   A: Crossbow
   B: Poison
   C: Axe
   D: She didn't – the original Sarah won

10. In *They Cloned Tyrone (2023),* what is Fontaine's job?

CLONES ALONE

1. *The Boys from Brazil (1978)* was based on a novel by which novelist?

2. Who directed *Multiplicity (1996)*?

3. At the end of *The 6th Day (2000)*, Adam Gibson's clone goes to live out his life in which South American country?

4. How old is the clone in *Godsend (2004)* before he starts to get visions?

5. Who wrote the novel that *Never Let Me Go (2010)* is based on?

6. In *Oblivion (2013)*, Jack repeatedly announces 'How can man die better, than facing fearful odds, for the ashes of his fathers, and the temples of his Gods?' What is the poem and poet that he is quoting?

7. Where was Henry Brogan, the protagonist of *Gemini Man (2019)*, born (and potentially raised)?

8. *Swan Song (2021)* stars Mahershala Ali and Naomie Harris, who previously appeared together in which film?

9. In her dream sequence at the start of *Dual (2022)*, what does Sarah start coughing up?

10. What is the name of Fontaine's neighbourhood in *They Cloned Tyrone (2023)*?

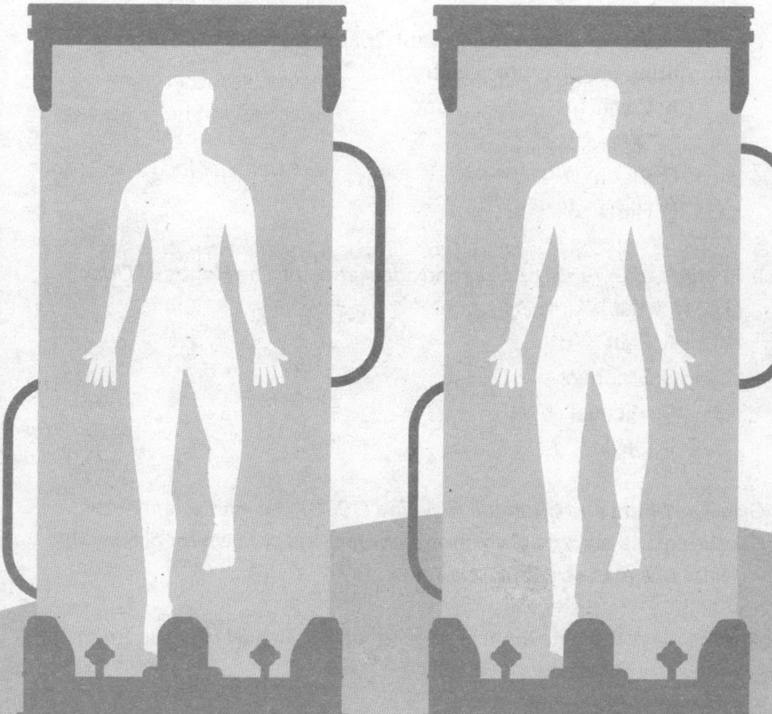

MEDICALLY DUBIOUS PRACTICES

It can be nerve-wracking to receive medical care. You know that laughter is the best medicine but you're sure it's supposed to be the *patient* who's laughing, and the practitioner insists on being called 'doctor' but is oddly evasive about where they trained, and the instruments look a lot like power tools and now you mention it what does a medical professional need with a Tesla coil anyway?

What we're saying is, it's probably fine, just try and answer these questions to take your mind off it.

1. In *The Hands of Orlac (1924)*, Paul Orlac has a hand transplant so he can continue to play which instrument?

   A: Violin

   B: Guitar

   C: Piano

   D: Harp

2. In *Mad Love (1935)*, the second adaptation of *The Hands of Orlac (1924)*, what is Orlac's first name?

   A: Paul

   B: Stephen

   C: Michael

   D: David

3. In *The Man Who Changed His Mind (1936)*, the mad scientist Dr Laurience is played by which actor who is best known for playing the *result* of a mad scientist's experiments?

4. Who plays the renowned brain surgeon Dr Michael Hfuhruhurr in *The Man with Two Brains (1983)*?

   A: Rick Moranis

   B: Steve Martin

   C: Robin Williams

   D: Bill Murray

5. In *Re-Animator (1985)*, the movie adaptation of H.P. Lovecraft's *Herbert West–Reanimator*, to which famously Lovecraftian university does Herbert West move to continue his studies?

6. What is the name of the experimental drug that allows Arnold Schwarzenegger's character to carry a baby to term in *Junior (1994)*?
   A: Probabiol
   B: Pregnamax
   C: Expectane
   D: Con-CV

7. Which former *Buffy the Vampire Slayer* actor plays a repo man for organ transplants in *Repo! The Genetic Opera (2008)*?
   A: James Marsters
   B: Anthony Head
   C: David Boreanaz
   D: Seth Green

8. In *Repo Men (2010)*, a repo man for artificial organs is forced to go on the run after he is given which artificial organ?
   A: Lung
   B: Kidney
   C: Heart
   D: Liver

9. Where is the 'wellness centre' in *A Cure for Wellness (2016)* situated?
   A: Germany
   B: Switzerland
   C: Sweden
   D: The Netherlands

10. In *Get Out (2017)*, how many times would Dean Armitage have voted for Obama (if he could)?

1. Paul Orlac loses use of his hands in *The Hands of Orlac (1924)* through what kind of accident?
   - A: Car accident
   - B: Train accident
   - C: Woodcutting accident
   - D: Skiing accident

2. Who played the sinister Doctor Gogol in *Mad Love (1935)*?

3. In *The Man Who Changed His Mind (1936)*, what habit gives away Dr Laurience's true identity when he takes control of Dick Haslewood's body?
   - A: Biting his nails
   - B: Drinking
   - C: Smoking
   - D: A stutter

4. What is the name of the disembodied brain that Dr Hfuhruhurr falls in love with in *The Man with Two Brains (1983)*? Her first name will do unless you are trying to show off.

5. Which actor, best known for playing multiple *Star Trek* roles, stars as Herbert West in *Re-Animator (1985)*?

6. *Junior (1994)* stars Danny DeVito and Arnold Schwarzenegger, who previously starred together in which other science fiction comedy?
7. Which famous socialite plays Amber Sweet in *Repo! The Genetic Opera (2008)*?
8. What is the name of the corporation that sells the artificial organs in *Repo Men (2010)*?
9. In *Get Out (2017)*, what is the name of the place Chris Washington is sent to when he is hypnotised?
10. In *Poor Things (2023)* who plays Victoria/Bella the adult woman who receives a brain transplant from her own fetus?

MEDICALLY DUBIOUS PRACTICES

1. What is the name of the recently executed killer who was the donor of *The Hands of Orlac (1924)*?

2. Who wrote the book that *Mad Love (1935)* and *The Hands of Orlac (1924)* are based on?

3. Who directed *The Man Who Changed His Mind (1936)*?

4. In *The Man with Two Brains (1983)*, which popular 80s talk show host is revealed to be 'The Elevator Killer'?

5. In *Re-Animator (1985)*, the first person to be brought back from the dead shares his name with which popular action movie villain?

6. Who plays the egg donor to Schwarzenegger's character in *Junior (1994)*?

7. What is the name of the highly sought-after drug secreted from corpses in *Repo! The Genetic Opera (2008)*?

8. What book is *Repo Men (2010)* based on?

9. In *A Cure for Wellness (2016)*, what animal receives life-restoring qualities from the water in the spa's aquifer?

10. In *Get Out (2017)*, Jim Hudson wants to have his brain transplanted into Chris Washington's because he wants which of his body parts?

QUICKFIRE ROUND: MATCH THE JEKYLLS & HYDES TO THE MOVIES!

While Frankenstein gets a lot of the glory, the truth is that Doctor Jekyll may be one of the most important practitioners of mad science in history. To start with, he discovered a way for actors to claim two pay cheques from the same movie.

1. *Dr. Jekyll and Mr. Hyde (1908)*
2. *Dr. Jekyll and Mr. Hyde (1912)*
3. *Dr. Jekyll and Mr. Hyde (1913)*
4. *Dr. Jekyll and Mr. Hyde (1920) (Dir. by J. Charles Haydon)*
5. *Dr. Jekyll and Mr. Hyde (1920) (Dir. By John S. Robertson)*
6. *Dr. Jekyll and Mr. Hyde (1931)*
7. *Dr. Jekyll and Mr. Hyde (1941)*
8. *Abbott and Costello Meet Dr. Jekyll and Mr. Hyde (1953)*
9. *The Strange Case of Dr. Jekyll and Mr. Hyde (1968)*
10. *Dr. Jekyll and Ms. Hyde (1995)*
11. *Dr. Jekyll and Mr. Hyde (2002)*
12. *Dr. Jekyll & Mr. Hyde (2008)*

A. *Boris Karloff and Eddie Parker*

B. *Dougray Scott*

C. *Fredric March*

D. *Hobart Bosworth*

E. *Jack Palance*

F. *James Cruze*

G. *John Barrymore*

H. *John Hannah*

I. *King Baggot*

J. *Sheldon Lewis*

K. *Spencer Tracy*

L. *Tim Daly and Sean Young*

MAD SCIENTISTS!

Real science does not happen in a rocket ship or a dystopian government building or even a parallel dimension. It happens in laboratories, secret ones, sometimes during thunderstorms.

It is the work of these dreamers, these visionaries, with their novelty teeth and their sticky-up hair and their eyes that seem to come just a little too far out of their head. You might call them mad, *mad* you say! But you'll see. Soon you will all see...

1. Rotwang, the mad scientist of *Metropolis (1927)*, has replaced which of his limbs with a mechanical prosthetic?

   A: Left hand

   B: Right hand

   C: Left foot

   D: Right foot

2. Dr Pretorius, the madder and more villainous counterpart to Frankenstein in *The Bride of Frankenstein (1935)*, toasts to a world of which two things?

   A: Freaks
   B: Geeks
   C: Gods
   D: Heroes
   E: Kings
   F: Madmen
   G: Men
   H: Mice
   I: Monsters
   J: Saints

3. Sidney Stratton, the inventor in *The Man in the White Suit (1951)*, was played by which Ealing comedy actor and Jedi?

4. When Andre Delambre tests the matter-transporter in *The Fly (1958)*, which *two* of his body parts are switched with that of a housefly?

5. Julius Kelp is the original star of *The Nutty Professor (1963)*, but what is the name of his charismatic alter ego?

6. Dr Strangelove of *Dr. Strangelove or: How I Learned to Stop Worrying and Love the Bomb (1964)* is played by Peter Sellers, but which of these other characters does he play in the film (select *all* the correct answers)?

   A: Lionel Mandrake

   B: Jack D. Ripper

   C: 'King' Kong

   D: Merk Muffley

7. Who plays Dr Emilio Lizardo, the evil mad scientist in *The Adventures of Buckaroo Banzai Across the 8th Dimension (1984)*?

   A: Jack Nicholson

   B: John Lithgow

   C: Michael Ironside

   D: William Atherton

8. *Ghostbusters (1984)* is full of mad scientists to a certain extent, but which ghostbuster does not have a doctorate?

   A: Egon Spengler

   B: Ray Stantz

   C: Peter Venkman

   D: Winston Zeddmore

9. In *Back to the Future (1985)* what is Doc Brown's first name?

10. Seth Brundle, the scientist in David Cronenberg's reimagining of *The Fly (1986)*, is played by which actor?

11. In *The Nutty Professor (1996)*, Sherman Klump originally creates his experimental formula as what?

    A: A love potion

    B: For weight loss

    C: Baldness prevention

    D: Intelligence booster

MAD SCIENTISTS!

1. Rotwang originally designs the iconic Maschinenmensch of *Metropolis (1927)* to resemble his lost love. What was her name?

2. In *The Bride of Frankenstein (1935)* which of Dr Pretorius' creations does he 'flatter' himself has a certain resemblance?

   A: The Queen
   B: The King
   C: The Archbishop
   D: The Devil

3. Why can the fabric Sidney Stratton invents in *The Man in the White Suit (1951)* only be white?

4. What is the first animal Andre Delambre puts through his matter-transporter in *The Fly (1958)*?

5. Who played Julius Kelp in *The Nutty Professor (1963)*?

6. What gender ratio does Dr Strangelove recommend for the underground shelters in *Dr. Strangelove or: How I Learned to Stop Worrying and Love the Bomb* (1964)?

7. Dr Emilio Lizardo, in *The Adventures of Buckaroo Banzai Across the 8th Dimension (1984)*, is controlled by which evil alien entity?

8. What two subjects does founding member Peter Venkman have PhDs in, in *Ghostbusters (1984)*?

9. What invention is Doc Brown working on when Marty finds him to try and get home in *Back to the Future (1985)*?

10. When Seth Brundle first attempts to teleport a baboon in *The Fly (1986)*, what is wrong with it when it reappears?

11. How many roles, including Sherman Klump and his counterpart, does Eddie Murphy play in *The Nutty Professor (1996)*?

    A: Five

    B: Six

    C: Seven

    D: Eight

MAD SCIENTISTS!

1. In *Metropolis (1927)*, who played the mad scientist Rotwang?

2. Who plays Dr Septimus Pretorius in *The Bride of Frankenstein (1935)*?

3. Which Scottish playwright wrote the stage play that would eventually become *The Man in the White Suit (1951)*?

4. What device does Andre Delambre's wife use to crush his head in *The Fly (1958)*?

5. Who wrote and directed *The Nutty Professor (1963)*?

6. In *Dr Strangelove or: How I Learned to Stop Worrying and Love the Bomb (1964)*, Dr Strangelove was an Anglicised name the doctor chose when he came to the USA. What was his original surname?

7. Where is Dr Emilio Lizardo incarcerated at the start of *The Adventures of Buckaroo Banzai Across the 8th Dimension (1984)*?

8. What does Egon Spengler collect in *Ghostbusters (1984)*?

9. Where was Doc Brown standing right before he had the idea for the flux capacitor in *Back to the Future (1985)*?

10. What is the name of the company funding Seth Brundle's research in *The Fly (1986)*?

11. What university does Sherman Klump, *The Nutty Professor (1996)*, work at?

ANSWERS

ROBOTS AND AI

HUMANOID ROBOTS

Caveman

1. *Jurassic Park*
2. C: Nicole Kidman
3. Acceptable answers: 'Attack ships on fire off the shoulder of Orion', 'C-beams glitter in the dark near the Tannhäuser Gate'
4. A: Kyle Reese
5. A: 29 August 1997
6. B: Station
7. B: Andrew
8. D: *Star Trek: Nemesis*
9. A Turing test
10. A Voight-Kampff test

Astronaut

1. A: Maria
2. Futureworld
3. Omni Consumer Products
4. C: 2029
5. B: Fembots
6. Osamu Tezuka
7. Joel Kinnaman
8. Because it is shot in the first person
9. Stanley Kubrick
10. D: Technologically Integrated Manservant

HUMANOID ROBOTS

Pan-Dimensional Star Baby

1. The word 'Robot' was not coined until the play *R.U.R.* was written in 1920

2. 'Love'

3. New food sources

4. A super soldier

5. T-800

6. *Supertoys Last All Summer Long*

7. Maren Eggert

8. Colin Farrell

9. Funki

10. He reads the dictionary

NON-HUMANOID ROBOTS

Caveman

1. B: His heart
2. B: Huey, Dewey and Louie
3. Johnny Five
4. D: ED-209
5. C: EMP
6. B: Superman
7. A: A spider
8. A fighter jet
9. B: Sigourney Weaver
10. B: Look after his dog

NON-HUMANOID ROBOTS

Astronaut

1. Harry Houdini
2. B: Italy
3. Superman
4. A: Box
5. C: *Runaway*
6. D: Jinx
7. Batteries
8. An antique copy of *Don Quixote*
9. 90%
10. C: A skin graft

NON-HUMANOID ROBOTS

Pan-Dimensional Star Baby

1. Acceptable answers include *The '?' Motorist*, *Questionmark Motorist* or *The Mad Motorist*, made in 1906

2. Bob Wayne

3. Ro-Man

4. Acceptable answers: *The Invisible Boy (1957), Hollywood Boulevard (1976), Heavy Metal (1981), Gremlins (1984), Earth Girls Are Easy (1988), Looney Tunes: Back in Action (2003)*

5. Martin Amis

6. An owl

7. *Chopping Mall (1986)*

8. Peter Weller

9. It has no name, it is just called 'Robot'

10. *Steel* by Richard Matheson

SUPERCOMPUTERS!

Caveman

1. C: 'Daisy Bell'
2. A: A bomb
3. B: Voyager 6
4. A: Tic-Tac-Toe
5. A: VIKI
6. 42
7. C: Emojis
8. Spike Jonze
9. To protect them from the robot uprising outside
10. B: The Entity

SUPERCOMPUTERS!

Astronaut

1. Douglas Rain
2. A: Guardian
3. Zero
4. C: To impregnate her
5. War Operation Plan Response
6. *Electric Dreams (1984)*
7. B: Miles Dyson
8. C: Kick me
9. D: Revolutionary Independence From Technology
10. A: To judge humanity

SUPERCOMPUTERS!

Pan-Dimensional Star Baby

1. SAL 9000
2. Joseph Sargent
3. Phenomenology
4. Dean Koontz
5. Zed
6. Earth
7. Samantha
8. John Cusack
9. Aries
10. James Corden

PREHISTORIC BEASTS

Caveman

1. A: Arthur Conan Doyle

2. C: Skull Island

3. A: It thaws out of the ice

4. C: A German U-boat

5. Isla Nublar

6. B: An Allosaurus

7. His brother

8. A: Sleestacks

9. Jason Statham

10. Earth

PREHISTORIC BEASTS

Astronaut

1. D: S.S. *Venture*
2. C: Rhedosaurus
3. B: Willis O'Brien
4. Gallimimus
5. *Tammy and the T-Rex (1994)*
6. *Super Mario Bros (1993)*
7. C: Bruce Baxter
8. Quantum Palaeontology
9. A: Megalodon
10. *A Quiet Place (2018)*

Pan-Dimensional Star Baby

1. *The Ghost of Slumber Mountain (1918)*
2. B: *The Giant Behemoth (1959)*
3. Merian C. Cooper or Ernest B. Schoedsack
4. He rides a rollercoaster
5. *The People That Time Forgot (1977)*
6. *We're Back! A Dinosaur's Story (1993)*
7. BD Wong (As Dr Henry Wu)
8. Whoopi Goldberg
9. A Sumatran rat monkey
10. Mills

MUTATIONS AND CREATIONS

Caveman

1. Boris Karloff
2. B: *Godzilla, King of the Monsters!*
3. C: Ants
4. C: Marlon Brando
5. Guillermo del Toro
6. Samuel L. Jackson
7. B: Formaldehyde
8. D: Dren
9. *Journey to the Centre of the Earth*
10. A: Dwayne 'The Rock' Johnson
11. Leonardo, Donatello, Raphael, Michelangelo

Astronaut

1. A: 1910

2. D: *Elko Maru*

3. Captain Nemo

4. B: The House of Pain

5. Mantises and Termites

6. C: Makos

7. *Parasite (2019)*

8. Adrien Brody

9. A video game

10. 1990

MUTATIONS AND CREATIONS

Pan-Dimensional Star Baby

1. Henry
2. *The Island of Lost Souls (1932)*
3. Ishirō Honda
4. The American Civil War
5. H.G. Wells
6. Mr Funny Shoes
7. Alzheimer's
8. A pig
9. Fred and Ginger
10. Dr Godwin Baxter

Caveman

1. B: Four minutes

2. A: A giant amoeba

3. C: The Golden Gate Bridge

4. Gizmo

5. *Arachnophobia (1990)*

6. B: Kevin Bacon

7. B: Electricity

8. A: A farewell party

9. Acceptable answers: Werewolf, Alien Beast, Mutants, Wraiths, Zombies, Reptilius, Clowns, Witches, Sexy Witches, Demons, Hell Lord, Angry Molesting Tree, Giant Snake, Deadites, Kevin, Mummy, The Bride, The Scarecrow Folk, Snowman, DragonBat, Vampires, Dismemberment Goblins, Sugarplum Fairy, Merman, The Reanimated, Unicorn, Huron, Sasquatch/Wendigo, Yeti, The Dolls, The Doctors, Zombie Redneck Torture Family, Jack O'Lantern, Giant, Twins

10. The Mariana Trench

NEW SPECIES

Astronaut

1. It was screened in 3D

2. Roger Corman

3. Stop motion

4. Don't expose them to bright light; don't get them wet; don't feed them after midnight

5. D: A coffin

6. B: Graboids

7. Daniel Clamp

8. Hud

9. C: Sigourney Weaver

10. Abe Sapien in *Hellboy (2004)*

Pan-Dimensional Star Baby

1. The Amazon

2. A one-man submarine

3. Six

4. Kingston Falls

5. It has no sex organs

6. Vibration detection

7. 'Genetic sunblock'

8. Something falling into the ocean

9. The whore, the athlete, the scholar and the fool (the virgin can die or survive, and so is not an acceptable answer here)

10. Occam Aerospace Research Centre

WE COME IN PEACE

Caveman

1. C: Mr Carpenter
2. David Bowie
3. A: Steven Spielberg
4. Extra-Terrestrial
5. A: Voyager 2
6. C: Max
7. McDonald's
8. B: Carl Sagan
9. A: South Africa
10. A: Seth Rogen
11. C: Abbott and Costello

WE COME IN PEACE

Astronaut

1. He switches off all electrical equipment on Earth (except for hospitals and aircraft in flight)

2. B: Water

3. Mashed potato

4. C: Reese's Pieces

5. Scott, Jenny's dead husband

6. B: Phaelon

7. Mysterious Alien Creature

8. Adolf Hitler

9. 'Prawns'

10. B: Her eye

11. Mahjong

WE COME IN PEACE

Pan-Dimensional Star Baby

1. *Army of Darkness (1992)*
2. Walter Tevis
3. *Firelight (1964)*
4. Chrysanthemums
5. 'Go very fast'
6. Paul Reubens
7. Jennifer Aniston
8. B: The Very Large Array
9. MNU or Multinational Unit are both acceptable answers
10. Twiki from *Buck Rogers in the 25th Century*
11. The Universal Language

CLOSE ENCOUNTERS OF THE SCARY KIND

Caveman

1. A: The Arctic
2. B: Bernard
3. D: Steve McQueen
4. A: Wildfire
5. A dog
6. H.R. Giger
7. C: Scarlett Johansson
8. Sleeps
9. B: Harry
10. A: Jean Jacket

CLOSE ENCOUNTERS OF THE SCARY KIND

Astronaut

1. *Who Goes There?* by John W. Campbell
2. The British American Rocket Group – changed from the British Experimental Rocket Group in the original TV serial
3. 'As long as the Arctic stays cold'
4. C: Because he is unmarried
5. A: Extreme heat
6. So that it will be "more docile and controllable"
7. C: Edgar
8. Glasgow
9. *Virus (1999)*
10. A shark
11. Looking at it directly

CLOSE ENCOUNTERS OF THE SCARY KIND

Pan-Dimensional Star Baby

1. It is electrocuted
2. Nigel Kneale
3. *Daughter of Horror* or *Dementia* are both acceptable answers.
4. Its blood is too alkaline
5. *The Hateful Eight (2015)*
6. Travis Walton
7. *Three – Species II (1998), Species III (2004),* and *Species: The Awakening (2007)*
8. Cake
9. 1983
10. The Horse in Motion, or Sallie Gardner at a Gallop are acceptable answers

FIRST CONTACT

ALIEN INVASION!

Caveman

1. A: *Invaders from Mars*
2. C: Washington D.C.
3. Pod people
4. C: Sunglasses
5. C: *The Midwich Cuckoos*
6. C: Trading cards
7. A: Elijah Wood
8. C: Tom Cruise
9. The Doctor, played by Jodie Whittaker ('Doctor Who' whilst technically incorrect, is also an acceptable answer...)
10. B: Drinking alcohol
11. He is caught in a time loop
12. A: Sound

Astronaut

1. B: William Cameron Menzies
2. B: Bacteria
3. Skyhook
4. Santa Mira
5. Kick ass and chew bubble gum
6. They have the same hair and eye colour
7. Jack Nicholson
8. Zeke's homemade drugs
9. Morgan Freeman
10. Guy Fawkes Night (Bonfire Night is also an acceptable answer)
11. Abbott
12. C: Legislators

ALIEN INVASION!

Pan-Dimensional Star Baby

1. Dan O'Bannon
2. Clayton Forrester
3. Solidified electricity
4. Capgras
5. Global warming
6. 1995
7. A Chihuahua
8. Ogilvy
9. Brewis
10. Blanks

QUICKFIRE ROUND: SPOT THE SPACESHIP! NAME THE MOVIE!

1. *Event Horizon (1997)*
2. *Forbidden Planet (1956)*
3. *Silent Running (1972)*
4. *2001: A Space Odyssey (1968)*
5. *Hitchhiker's Guide to the Galaxy (2005)*
6. *Interstellar (2014)*
7. *Passengers (2016)*
8. *Sunshine (2007)*
9. *Pitch Black (2000)*
10. *Lost in Space (1998)*

FROM EARTH TO THE MOON

Caveman

1. In the eye
2. B: Robert A. Heinlein
3. C: 2090s
4. A: An Apollo module
5. C: Because it is made of cheese
6. C: 'The One and Only' by Chesney Hawkes
7. C: Apollo 18
8. D: The Hubble Telescope
9. C: Calvin
10. A little girl
11. A: A megastructure
12. A: World War 3

FROM EARTH TO THE MOON

Astronaut

1. Georges Méliès
2. A: Woody Woodpecker
3. Gene Hackman
4. David Bowie
5. An early warning missile detection system
6. C: Armadyne Corp
7. Kessler
8. D: *Goodnight Moon*
9. It is the first South Korean film set in space
10. *Moon 44 (1990)*

SPACE EXPLORATION

FROM EARTH TO THE MOON

Pan-Dimensional Space Baby

1. Selenites
2. Because they used too much fuel during the landing
3. X-RV
4. Helium 3
5. Freedom and Liberty
6. Diego Luna
7. *Apollo 13 (1995)*
8. *Message from Space (1978)*
9. Spaceship Victory
10. A white dwarf

Caveman

1. B: A bigger monolith
2. D: Forests
3. B: Sean Connery
4. A: Europa
5. B: Proxima Centauri
6. C: *Mission to Mars* and F: *Red Planet*
7. A: Ice Cube
8. Mercury
9. A: Turns them into zombies
10. D: A solar storm
11. B: Potatoes
12. B: His father

SPACE EXPLORATION

OUR SOLAR SYSTEM

Astronaut

1. B: Three
2. American Airlines
3. C: Io
4. Nuclear fusion, turning it into a star
5. Gravity drive
6. A Disney theme park attraction
7. Pathfinder
8. Snake Plissken
9. Realign the heat shields
10. Aurora Mars Mission 2
11. An alien lifeform
12. Mark Watney
13. C: A baboon

Pan-Dimensional Space Baby

1. Excelsior
2. Also sprach Zarathustra
3. Valley Forge
4. Doctor Lazarus
5. 2064 and 3001
6. His suit's oxygen supply
7. Matriarchal
8. Sydney
9. Corrigan
10. The Lima Project

SPACE EXPLORATION

DEEP SPACE

Caveman

1. A: *The Tempest*
2. D: Queen
3. David Lynch
4. C: Robinson
5. "Never surrender!" – *Galaxy Quest (1999)*
6. A: Light
7. B: George Clooney
8. A: Slartibartfast
9. B: Down
10. C: 23 years
11. D: Spice
12. B: Idaho
13. B: Austin Butler
14. C: A mouse

Astronaut

1. Frank Drebin
2. Thals
3. Stanisław Lem
4. Surfs on it
5. B: American Football
6. Patrick Stewart
7. C: Currency
8. C: Dick Tufeld
9. '...by the Sons of Warvan, you shall be avenged.' ('...what a savings' is also acceptable) from *Galaxy Quest (1999)*
10. A shine job
11. Arrakis
12. C. A poison needle
13. Harkonnen
14. Josh Brolin

SPACE EXPLORATION

DEEP SPACE

Pan-Dimensional Space Baby

1. Altair IV
2. *Planet of the Vampires*
3. Buster Crabbe
4. Alejandro Jodorowsky
5. United Global Space Force
6. A beryllium sphere
7. The Point of View Gun
8. Arkanar
9. Formics
10. Gargantua
11. He spits
12. 'Weapon of Choice' by Fatboy Slim

BACKWARDS IN TIME

Caveman

1. C: Mark Twain
2. A: Hypnosis
3. B: 88 miles per hour
4. A: Wyld Stallyns
5. A: 1885
6. D: Terry Gilliam
7. B: The Hundred Years' War
8. B: Henry DeTamble
9. C: 1986
10. C: Chevy Chase
11. A: Seattle Magazine

BACKWARDS IN TIME

Astronaut

1. Bing Crosby

2. C: *12 Monkeys (1995)*

3. Twin Pines Mall

4. Lone Pine Mall

5. Acceptable answers: Napoleon, Billy the Kid, Socrates, Sigmund Freud, Genghis Khan, Joan of Arc, Abraham Lincoln, Beethoven

6. B: Clint Eastwood

7. Jeffrey Goines

8. A: A bifocal lens

9. Zero. Rachel McAdams has appeared in four movies that involve time travel - *The Time Traveller's Wife, Midnight in Paris, Doctor Strange* and *About Time*, but her character never time travels in any of them

10. To save his high school sweetheart

Pan-Dimensional Star-Baby

1. He gets hit by a car
2. A solar eclipse
3. His own death
4. Vulcan
5. San Dimas High
6. ZZ Top
7. 1914-1918, World War One
8. 1991
9. An arm
10. A boat

FORWARDS IN TIME

Caveman

1. A: Morlocks and D: Eloi
2. D: 2024
3. B: A time portal
4. A: H.G. Wells and D: Jack the Ripper
5. B: The USS *Philadelphia*
6. B: Eight years
7. B: 2015
8. A: 2032
9. C: Guy Pearce
10. C: 500 years

FORWARDS IN TIME

Astronaut

1. An 'Atomic satellite'
2. An X-80 experimental aircraft
3. C: Alpha Centauri
4. C: The non-return key
5. B: 1943
6. Sarah Jessica Parker
7. C: *Jaws 19*
8. John Spartan
9. He is his great-grandson
10. St. God's Memorial Hospital

FORWARDS IN TIME

Pan-Dimensional Star Baby

1. George

2. The Citadel

3. 2071

4. McDonald's

5. Santa Paula, California

6. *Starsky & Hutch*

7. Gray's Sports Almanac

8. San Angeles

9. Vox

10. Not Sure

CHANGING HISTORY

Caveman

1. C: Jean-Claude Van Damme
2. A: Firefighter
3. C: A storage facility
4. D: Ashton Kutcher
5. C: A ferry
6. A: The gents' toilet
7. A: Joseph Gordon-Levitt and E: Bruce Willis
8. B: Get a girlfriend
9. A: Inversion

Mini round – Time Loops!

1. A: 'I Got You Babe' by Sonny & Cher
2. B: Chicago
3. D: Heathrow
4. A: A wedding

CHANGING HISTORY

Astronaut

1. The stock market crash
2. B: Lung cancer
3. A device that can reduce the weight of an object
4. B: Snow White
5. The Editors
6. To get around the surveillance systems in the future
7. Their child's conception
8. Stalsk-12

Mini round – Time Loops!

1. Punxsutawney
2. C: Teacher
3. Angel of Verdun
4. Roy

Pan-Dimensional Star Baby

1. 2004
2. 'The Nightingale'
3. A much bigger box/time machine
4. An Emergency Room
5. Ray the Great
6. The Rainmaker
7. Once
8. He is never given a name, the credits list him as 'The Protagonist'

Mini round – Time Loops!

1. February 2nd
2. The last eight minutes of dead people's memories
3. The Louvre
4. November 9th

VIRTUAL REALITIES

Caveman

1. C: Construction Worker and G: Spy - The correct answers can be inserted into the question in either order.

2. B: A chimpanzee

3. C: Sadistic, Intelligent, Dangerous

4. Jim Carrey

5. A: The red pill

6. A: 1937

7. D: Jump off a building

8. B: Spinning a spinning top

9. C: OASIS

Astronaut

1. *We Can Remember it for You Wholesale*
2. Every telephone on the planet rings simultaneously
3. Russell Crowe
4. C: Burbank
5. Batteries
6. A: Realists
7. 2024
8. *Abre los Ojos (1997)* or *Open Your Eyes*
9. Lacuna
10. B: Four
11. Parzival
12. Victory

VIRTUAL REALITIES

Pan-Dimensional Space Baby

1. Carl Hauser
2. Stephen King
3. Peter Weir
4. *Johnny Mnemonic (1995)*
5. Thomas A. Anderson. Thomas Anderson is an acceptable answer.
6. The spine
7. *Simulacron-3* by Daniel F. Galouye
8. 'Non, je ne regrette rien'
9. C: *E.T. The Extra-Terrestrial (1982)*

The following films are referenced in *Ready Player One* as below:

A: *Monty Python and the Holy Grail (1975)* -
The Holy Hand Grenade appears.

B: *Smokey and the Bandit (1977)* -
Shoto's car is taken from this movie.

D: *Star Trek II: The Wrath of Khan (1982)* -
Halliday's coffin is based on Spock's in this film.

E: *Back to the Future (1985)* -
Parzival's car is a flying DeLorean.

F: *Big Trouble in Little China (1986)* -
The truck Kurt Russell drove in this movie appears in one scene.

G: *Robocop (1987)* -
Robocop is one of the avatars in the film's opening montage.

10. The Kaufmann House

OTHER REALMS

Caveman

1. B: Under his ranch
2. A: Atlantis
3. B: Rabbit
4. C: An inch a week
5. C: Brain
6. B: A grocery store clerk
7. C: The Priest
8. A: Mexico
9. C: The Shimmer
10. B: A housing estate

OTHER REALMS

Astronaut

1. B: Murania
2. Arne Saknussemm
3. A: The Tethered
4. A spider
5. *Proteus*
6. Jack and Lydia kiss
7. *Roadside Picnic* by Arkady and Boris Strugatsky
8. Gareth Edwards
9. Cassie
10. A: A cuckoo

OTHER REALMS

Pan-Dimensional Space Baby

1. Radium
2. Iceland
3. *Get Out (2017)*
4. Butch
5. Isaac Asimov
6. Igoe
7. Chernobyl
8. Six years
9. Jeff VanderMeer
10. Number 9

Caveman

1. C: 1945
2. Joan Collins
3. B: 1964
4. C: Rudyard Kipling
5. A: On a train
6. B: 125
7. D: A comet
8. C: Chris Pine
9. The Beatles
10. D: A launderette

INFINITE DIMENSIONS!

Astronaut

1. *It Can't Happen Here*

2. John Wyndham

3. Wallis Simpson

4. John Travolta

5. "Nobody expects the Spanish inquisition!"

6. B: Al Gore

7. Blue

8. A Rubix cube

9. C: Ed Sheeran

10. An Everything Bagel

Pan-Dimensional Star Baby

1. Sebastian Shaw

2. Nobody had ever succeeded in climbing Mount Everest.

3. Switzerland and the Vatican

4. Chocolates

5. She is hit by a van in one, and falls down a flight of stairs in the other.

6. Multiverse Authority

7. Roswell

8. 42

9. Lowestoft

10. Makes herself sneeze with a duster

BIG BROTHER IS WATCHING YOU

Caveman

1. C: Nadsat
2. George Lucas
3. C: Frankenstein
4. A: Oceania
5. D: Christmas
6. E: Nitro
7. Mega City One
8. Guy Fawkes
9. C: The Fishes
10. A: Peach Trees

BIG BROTHER IS WATCHING YOU

Astronaut

1. Milk-Plus
2. C: LUH 3417
3. B: The World Crash of '79
4. B: The Ministry of Truth
5. Archibald Buttle
6. Archibald Tuttle
7. Richard Bachman
8. The Republic of Gilead
9. '...and okay for you'
10. B: Hugo Weaving
11. Kee
12. Slo-Mo

BIG BROTHER IS WATCHING YOU

Pan-Dimensional Star Baby

1. Peter Cheyney
2. The Ludovico technique
3. A Wookiee
4. 40 points
5. Richard Burton
6. 'Aquarela do Brasil'
7. 2017
8. Harold Pinter
9. Joseph
10. 'Fingermen'
11. P.D. James
12. Six

EVERYTHING IS FINE! (HONEST)

Caveman

1. B: Paper burns
2. A: Soylent Red and B: Soylent Yellow
3. C: 30
4. Taco Bell
5. C: Titan
6. C: Gun Kata
7. Three
8. B: Pathogens
9. C: One year
10. Abnegation - Selfless,
    Amity - Peaceful,
    Candor - Honest,
    Dauntless - Brave,
    Erudite - Intelligent

EVERYTHING IS FINE! (HONEST)

Astronaut

1. B: *Tales of Mystery and Imagination* by Edgar Allen Poe
2. B: Plankton
3. Carousel
4. Seashells
5. B: 30.2 years
6. A: Libria
7. C: John Anderton
8. C: His liver
9. C: Amanda Seyfried (born 3 December 1985)
10. A: Chicago

EVERYTHING IS FINE! (HONEST)

Pan-Dimensional Star Baby

1. Wings Over the World
2. Oscar Werner
3. 20 billion people
4. 5
5. Edgar Friendly
6. Swimming
7. Prozium
8. A pair of scissors
9. Tom Lincoln
10. *Insurgent (2015)* and *Allegiant (2016)*

CLIMATE CATASTROPHE!

Caveman

1. C: Solar eclipse
2. B: Nuclear testing
3. B: A new ice age
4. Kevin Costner
5. C: Los Angeles
6. 2009
7. A: Aurochs
8. C: Train
9. Gerard Butler
10. C: Miami

Astronaut

1. B: A nearby quarry
2. C: *The Daily Express*
3. Six
4. Dirt
5. Roland Emmerich
6. John Cusack
7. Bathtub
8. Tilda Swinton
9. B: The Burj Khalifa
10. Hugh Jackman

THE END OF THE WORLD! (AND WHAT COMES NEXT...)

CLIMATE CATASTROPHE!

Pan-Dimensional Star Baby

1. New York
2. "World Saved" and "World Doomed"
3. Paul Newman
4. Mount Everest
5. New York Public Library
6. B: Neutrinos
7. Quvenzhané Wallis
8. A polar bear
9. Dutch Boy
10. Lisa Joy

Caveman

1. Men
2. B: Asia
3. George A. Romero
4. A: Musician
5. B: Scotland
6. B: Julianne Moore
7. *Star Trek (2009)*
8. C: The candidates must not confer
9. D: Mark Wahlberg
10. Japan

THE END OF THE WORLD! (AND WHAT COMES NEXT...)

PANDEMIC FEVER!

Astronaut

1. *The Death of Grass* by John Christopher
2. D: Trixie
3. B: Daniel Defoe
4. A phone
5. Reaper
6. An ophthalmologist
7. One, avoid the infected at all costs. Two, disinfect anything they've touched in the last 24 hours. Three, the sick are already dead, they can't be saved.
8. Colin Salmon
9. A: Bats and D: Pigs
10. Wes Anderson

Pan-Dimensional Star Baby

1. Masculitis
2. Roger Whittaker
3. Evans City
4. Gabriel García Márquez
5. Respiratory
6. Neil Marshall
7. José Saramago
8. Turtle Beach, Texas
9. DATAPREV
10. Forsythia
11. Chief

AFTER THE END

Caveman

1. B: Melbourne, Australia
2. C: Blood
3. C: Oil shortages
4. C: Steve Guttenberg
5. C: Sheffield
6. Kevin Costner
7. Cormac McCarthy
8. A: A Bible
9. Cornettos
10. B: Water

Astronaut

1. Fred Astaire

2. D: 2024

3. Rockatansky

4. Nicholas Meyer

5. B: *Warriors of the Wasteland*

6. B: Move it to another room in the house

7. C: By performing Shakespearean plays

8. Viggo Mortensen

9. An iPod

10. To supply a blood transfusion

AFTER THE END

Pan-Dimensional Star Baby

1. USS *Sawfish*
2. Harlan Ellison
3. A Pursuit Special
4. Lawrence
5. The Templars
6. Ten years
7. General Bethlehem
8. Charlize Theron
9. Alcatraz
10. Acceptable answers: Toast, Capable, the Dag, Cheedo, and Angharad.

Caveman

1. B: Vampires
2. C: Radiation from a crashed space probe
3. C: The Family
4. When there's no more room in Hell
5. D: Chimpanzees
6. B: The Winchester
7. B: ZomCon
8. Bill Murray's
9. C: United Nations
10. C: Fungus

THE END OF THE WORLD! (AND WHAT COMES NEXT…)

ZOMBIES

Astronaut

1. *I Am Legend* by Richard Matheson

2. Barbra and Johnny

3. The USSR and China

4. Tom Savini

5. Christopher Eccleston

6. *Spaced*

7. Billy Connolly

8. B: Mad Cow Disease

9. Max Brooks

10. Hungries

11. A: Seoul

Pan-Dimensional Star Baby

1. Vincent Price
2. Zero
3. Dodger Stadium
4. Monroeville Mall
5. St Thomas' Hospital
6. 'If You Leave Me Now' by Chicago, and 'Don't Stop Me Now' by Queen
7. Willard
8. Tallahassee
9. South Korea
10. Melanie
11. *Seoul Station*

THE END OF THE WORLD! (AND WHAT COMES NEXT...)

SPACE COLLISION

Caveman

1. C: Lexell's Comet
2. A: Genesis
3. C: An accidental rocket explosion
4. Sean Connery
5. C: Oil rig workers
6. Morgan Freeman
7. C: 70 miles
8. B: Jupiter
9. A: The survival shelter is in Greenland
10. C: Six months

Astronaut

1. D: Bellus

2. B: Zyra

3. C: *Death Comes from Outer Space*

4. Orpheus

5. A: Aerosmith

6. Extinction Level Event

7. Steve Carrell and Keira Knightley

8. Cixin Liu

9. Tampa, Florida

10. C: $140 trillion

THE END OF THE WORLD! (AND WHAT COMES NEXT...)

SPACE COLLISION

Pan-Dimensional Star Baby

1. *Omega: The Last Days of the World* by Camille Flammarion

2. Sidney Stanton

3. John MacLaren

4. 'Hercules' and 'Peter the Great'

5. Mir

6. Messiah

7. Matilda

8. MOSS

9. *The Hammer of God*

10. Bronteroc

THE END OF THE WORLD! (AND WHAT COMES NEXT...)

NOOBODY SAW THIS COMING!

Caveman

1. D: Alfred Hitchcock
2. C: Orange
3. A: Project Flashlight
4. France
5. Dragons
6. C: Stops spinning
7. C: A pharmacy
8. A: M. Night Shyamalan
9. A: English
10. B: Phoners
11. B: Cold-blooded creatures

THE END OF THE WORLD! (AND WHAT COMES NEXT...)

NOOBODY SAW THIS COMING!

Astronaut

1. Rod Taylor

2. *The Wonderful Wizard of Oz*

3. New Zealand

4. D: Clown

5. A: Bamburgh Castle

6. 'Unobtainium'

7. Maine

8. B: Plant toxins

9. *Pontypool Changes Everything* by Tony Burgess

10. C: 'Raggedy Man'

11. C: Gertie

Pan-Dimensional Star Baby

1. Daphne du Maurier

2. 'The Vortex'

3. They were each at the moment of death when the effect took place

4. *Alien: Resurrection (1997)*

5. *Star Wars: The Empire Strikes Back (1980)*

6. They have pacemakers

7. *The Shawshank Redemption (1994)* and *The Green Mile (1999)*

8. Paris

9. Terms of endearment, baby talk and rhetorical discourse.

10. Kashwak

11. Agatha 616

QUICKFIRE ROUND: MATCH THE INVISIBLE MAN!

The Invisible Man (1933)	Claude Rains
The Invisible Man Returns (1940)	Vincent Price
The Invisible Woman (1940)	Virginia Bruce
Invisible Agent (1942)	Jon Hall
Abbot & Costello Meet the Invisible Man (1951)	Arthur Franz
The Amazing Transparent Man (1960)	Douglas Kennedy
Memoirs of an Invisible Man (1992)	Chevy Chase
Hollow Man (2000)	Kevin Bacon
The Invisible Man (2020)	Oliver Jackson-Cohen

Caveman

1. B: Mouse

2. David Cronenberg

3. B: Christopher Walken

4. C: The President of the United States

5. B: He is albino

6. A: Auto mechanic

7. D: 2 minutes

8. C: Landlady

9. D: The Big Bang

10. C: 23

THE MIND UNLEASHED

Astronaut

1. A bakery
2. C: 237
3. C: Touches them
4. Christopher Plummer
5. Jeff Goldblum
6. B: Portuguese
7. Nicolas Cage
8. United States Senator
9. Taiwan
10. *Unbreakable (2000)*

Pan-Dimensional Star Baby

1. Cliff Robertson
2. Ephemerol
3. Greg Stillson
4. Thornhill College
5. She is struck by lightning
6. A brain tumour
7. 08:09
8. NZT-48
9. Pregnant women
10. D: Mr Glass

INCREDIBLE SUPERPOWERS

Caveman

1. C: Jack Griffin
2. Krypton
3. D: Drew Barrymore
4. C: A pink tutu
5. C: American football
6. B: Paladins
7. C: Nick Gant
8. B: Hydrogen
9. B: Simon Pegg
10. A: Kansas

INCREDIBLE SUPERPOWERS

Astronaut

1. James Whale
2. Smallville
3. Pyrokinesis
4. D: Tromaville
5. A train crash
6. Hayden Christensen
7. B: The Division
8. The Minutemen
9. Monty Python
10. C: Pieces of his spaceship

INCREDIBLE SUPERPOWERS

Pan-Dimensional Star Baby

1. C: 'I meddled in things that man must leave alone.'
2. Kirk Alyn
3. 'The Shop'
4. Elijah Prince
5. The Grand Canyon
6. Precognition
7. Jon Osterman
8. For an alien spaceship to crash into class 10c
9. *Super (2010)*
10. Peter Dinklage

Caveman

1. Adolf Hitler
2. B: 3
3. C: RePet
4. A: Adam
5. A: 1978
6. A: New York
7. Will Smith
8. B: Jack
9. C: Karen Gillan
10. B: John Boyega

CLONES ALONE

Astronaut

1. B: Because the original figure's father died when he was 13
2. C: Doug
3. Arnold Schwarzenegger
4. Robert De Niro
5. Andrew Garfield - Charlie Rowe,
   Keira Knightley - Ella Purnell,
   Carey Mulligan - Isobel Melkie-Small,
   Matt Smith - Tristan Christopher
6. A: Titan
7. Three
8. B: To replace him when he dies
9. B: Poison
10. Drug dealer

CLONES ALONE

Pan-Dimensional Star Baby

1. Ira Levin
2. Harold Ramis
3. Argentina
4. Eight years old
5. Kazuo Ishiguro
6. 'Horatius' by Thomas Babington Macaulay
7. Philadelphia
8. *Moonlight (2016)*
9. Pennies
10. The Glen

MEDICALLY DUBIOUS PRACTICES

Caveman

1. C: Piano
2. B: Stephen
3. Boris Karloff
4. B: Steve Martin
5. Miskatonic University
6. C: Expectane
7. B: Anthony Head
8. C: Heart
9. B: Switzerland
10. Three times

MEDICALLY DUBIOUS PRACTICES

Astronaut

1. B: Train accident
2. Peter Lorre
3. C: Smoking
4. Anne Uumellmahaye
5. Jeffrey Combs
6. *Twins (1988)*
7. Paris Hilton
8. The Union
9. The Sunken Place
10. Emma Stone

MEDICALLY DUBIOUS PRACTICES

Pan-Dimensional Star Baby

1. Vasseur
2. Maurice Renard
3. Robert Stevenson
4. Merv Griffin
5. Hans Gruber
6. Emma Thompson
7. Zydrate
8. *The Repossession Mambo* by Eric Garcia
9. Eels
10. His eyes

QUICKFIRE ROUND: MATCH THE JEKYLLS & HYDES TO THE MOVIES!

Dr. Jekyll and Mr. Hyde (1908)	Hobart Bosworth
Dr. Jekyll and Mr. Hyde (1912)	James Cruze
Dr. Jekyll and Mr. Hyde (1913)	King Baggot
Dr. Jekyll and Mr. Hyde (1920) (Dir. by J. Charles Haydon)	Sheldon Lewis
Dr. Jekyll and Mr. Hyde (1920) (Dir. By John S. Robertson)	John Barrymore
Dr. Jekyll and Mr. Hyde (1931)	Fredric March
Dr. Jekyll and Mr. Hyde (1941)	Spencer Tracy
Abbott and Costello Meet Dr. Jekyll and Mr. Hyde (1953)	Boris Karloff and Eddie Parker
The Strange Case of Dr. Jekyll and Mr. Hyde (1968)	Jack Palance
Dr. Jekyll and Ms. Hyde (1995)	Tim Daly and Sean Young
Dr. Jekyll and Mr. Hyde (2002)	John Hannah
Dr. Jekyll & Mr. Hyde (2008)	Dougray Scott

MAD SCIENTISTS!

Caveman

1. B: Right hand
2. C: Gods and I: Monsters
3. Alec Guinness
4. His head and his arm
5. Buddy Love
6. A: Lionel Mandrake and D: Merk Muffley
7. B: John Lithgow
8. D: Winston Zeddmore
9. Emmett
10. Jeff Goldblum
11. B: For weight loss

MAD SCIENTISTS!

Astronaut

1. Hel

2. D: The Devil

3. Because it won't absorb dye

4. A cat

5. Jerry Lewis

6. 10:1 female to male.

7. Lord John Whorfin

8. Parapsychology and psychology

9. A mindreading machine

10. It is inside out

11. C: Seven

MAD SCIENTISTS!

Pan-Dimensional Star Baby

1. Rudolf Klein-Rogge
2. Ernest Thesiger
3. Roger MacDougall
4. A hydraulic press
5. Jerry Lewis
6. Merkwürdigliebe (German for 'Strangelove')
7. Trenton Home for the Criminally Insane
8. Moulds and fungus
9. On the toilet
10. Bartok Science Industries
11. Wellman College

NOTES